SO-BCN-963

Vivienne Roseby, PhD
Janet Johnston, PhD
Bettina Gentner, LCSW
Erin Moore, LCSW

A Safe Place to Grow
A Group Treatment Manual for Children in Conflicted, Violent, and Separating Homes

Pre-publication
REVIEWS,
COMMENTARIES,
EVALUATIONS . . .

"The prevalence and anguish of children growing up in high-conflict or violent homes creates an urgent need for sound treatment methods that support their healthy development in the face of stresses and vulnerabilities that cycle for generations. Yet the complex developmental challenges posed by conflicted and/or hostile family environments often elude effective treatment. The group model detailed by these authors takes its place as a giant among former efforts. Developmentally appropriate, culturally sensitive materials are simultaneously creative and grounded in evidence-based theory and research. The authors draw from fantasy and role-play centering around a beloved children's book, puppets, and real situations children encounter to help them move beyond constricted worldviews steeped in safety concerns, and test healthier ways of thinking, feeling, and interacting with parents and significant others. The authors prove once again they know children, conflict, violence, and intervention better than almost anybody else practicing today."

Marsha Kline Pruett, PhD, MSL
Associate Professor in Law
and Psychiatry and the Yale Child
Study Center, Yale University
School of Medicine

More pre-publication
REVIEWS, COMMENTARIES, EVALUATIONS . . .

"**R**oseby, Johnston, Gentner, and Moore provide practitioners with a sensitive, practical, and detailed guide for working with children in high-conflict, violent, or separating families when what needs to be changed—parents' out-of-control emotions—cannot. This session-by-session manual is full of creative exercises designed to reach children emotionally, offer them perspective, and alter their behavior. The ultimate goal is to help children move forward with their 'job'—being a kid, in tragic cases where parents fail to do their job of protecting, nurturing, and guiding children. Highly recommended for any clinician working with children from high-conflict, separated, or divorced families."

Robert Emery, PhD
Professor of Psychology,
Director of the Center for Children,
Families, and the Law, University
of Virginia, Charlottesville; Author,
The Truth About Children and Divorce

"*A Safe Place to Grow* is an updated and expanded version of the authors' earlier book that describes a model for working with children who have experienced chronic conflict or violence in their families. This edition of the manual includes refinements made to the treatment model along with two valuable additions. The model has been expanded so it is now applicable for children from about five to fourteen years of age. The authors' recommendations about adapting the model for multiethnic communities are a particularly important addition to the divorce literature, given the increasing diversity of our communities.

Divorce challenges even the most resilient children. Growing up in a high-conflict or violent family creates additional stresses and burdens. The group treatment model described by these respected clinicians is a meaningful way to begin addressing the risks and profound concerns identified in the literature for these children. Building on a review of how ongoing conflict affects children, the authors outline a model for working with the preoccupations, fears, and concerns that influence how children see the world. The therapeutic goals of the model are linked to the developmental implications for children.

Session-by-session, the goals, activities, format, and group rules are outlined. The clinical notes that accompany the text will assist readers in implementing this sophisticated intervention designed to foster resilience and build coping repertoires. Many of the activities, using commonly available materials, are also suitable for individual work with children. Scripts provided for handling issues that typically arise in group work with children will be useful for clinicians—particularly the sage advice about ways of managing disruptive behavior.

A Safe Place to Grow links research, theory, and practical strategies for supporting children who are coping with parent conflict and violence. The book is an important contribution to the divorce literature and a valuable resource for clinicians."

Rhonda Freeman, MSW, RSW
Director, Families in Transition,
Family Service Association of Toronto

More pre-publication
REVIEWS, COMMENTARIES, EVALUATIONS . . .

"This superb book captures the suffering, the bewilderment, and the hypervigilance of children who have witnessed parental fighting or have themselves been victims of violence. It provides the clinician with new ways of restoring the developmental processes that have been disrupted in the children and their families. Based on many years of clinical experience followed by scrupulous assessment, the authors propose that group experience, as described in this manual, is able to successfully reach children whose traumatic experiences with adults have rendered them far too fearful to make use of traditional one-to-one treatment. Having seen many instances of the fear of adults and the distrust that such children carry inside them and the many ways that their affects are frozen and almost robot-like, I appreciate the remarkable techniques which these authors have developed.

Written in a user-friendly style, the authors offer group programs for children of different ages coming from different cultures. The groups have been conducted in Spanish and English and have included children from Caucasian, Asian, African-American, and Hispanic families with appropriate modification to suit the demands of the different cultures. The group program includes puppets, drawing materials, and a wide range of simple, inexpensive paraphernalia. Each group meeting spells out the goals of that meeting, materials to be used, and step-by-step procedures.

It is primarily in the program that the imagination of the authors and their remarkable intuition regarding the needs of these traumatized children shows. At its simplest level, one game the children play in order to engender trust in each other. Each group includes shared snacks as symbolic tokens of the leader's interest. Each meeting ends which invitations to the children to express freely what they liked and did not like about the meeting on that day. This too permits the children to express their opinions without fear of reprisal.

This book is a groundbreaking contribution that significantly enlarges our capacity to help thousands of children who have been traumatized by witnessing or experiencing violence in their families."

Judith Wallerstein, PhD
Divorce Researcher; Author,
The Unexpected Legacy of Divorce;
Founder, the Judith Wallerstein Center
for the Family in Transition

HMTP

The Haworth Maltreatment and Trauma Press®
An Imprint of The Haworth Press, Inc.
New York • London • Oxford

NOTES FOR PROFESSIONAL LIBRARIANS
AND LIBRARY USERS

This is an original book title published by The Haworth Maltreatment and Trauma Press®, an imprint of The Haworth Press, Inc. Unless otherwise noted in specific chapters with attribution, materials in this book have not been previously published elsewhere in any format or language.

CONSERVATION AND PRESERVATION NOTES

All books published by The Haworth Press, Inc., and its imprints are printed on certified pH neutral, acid-free book grade paper. This paper meets the minimum requirements of American National Standard for Information Sciences-Permanence of Paper for Printed Material, ANSI Z39.48-1984.

A Safe Place to Grow
A Group Treatment Manual for Children in Conflicted, Violent, and Separating Homes

A Safe Place to Grow
A Group Treatment Manual for Children in Conflicted, Violent, and Separating Homes

Vivienne Roseby, PhD
Janet Johnston, PhD
Bettina Gentner, LCSW
Erin Moore, LCSW

HMTP

The Haworth Maltreatment and Trauma Press®
An Imprint of The Haworth Press, Inc.
New York • London • Oxford

For more information on this book or to order, visit
http://www.haworthpress.com/store/product.asp?sku=5488

or call 1-800-HAWORTH (800-429-6784) in the United States and Canada
or (607) 722-5857 outside the United States and Canada

or contact orders@HaworthPress.com

Published by

The Haworth Maltreatment and Trauma Press®, an imprint of The Haworth Press, Inc., 10 Alice Street, Binghamton, NY 13904-1580.

© 2005 by Vivienne Roseby, Janet R. Johnston, Bettina Gentner, and Erin Moore. All rights reserved. No part of this work may be reproduced or utilized in any form or by any means, electronic or mechanical, including photocopying, microfilm, and recording, or by any information storage and retrieval system, without permission in writing from the publisher. Printed in the United States of America.

Second edition of V. Roseby and J. R. Johnston, *High-Conflict, Violent, and Separating Families: A Group Treatment Manual for School-Age Children* (New York: The Free Press, 1997).

Original illustrations by Jose Lott.

Cover design by Lora Wiggins.

Library of Congress Cataloging-in-Publication Data

A safe place to grow : a group treatment manual for children in conflicted, violent, and separating homes / Vivienne Roseby . . . [et al.].
   p. cm.
  Includes bibliographical references and index.
  ISBN-13: 978-0-7890-2768-9 (hard : alk. paper)
  ISBN-10: 0-7890-2768-2 (hard : alk. paper)
  ISBN-13: 978-0-7890-2769-6 (soft : alk. paper)
  ISBN-10: 0-7890-2769-0 (soft : alk. paper)
  1. Problem families—Psychological aspects. 2. Abused children—Counseling of. 3. Children of abused wives—Counseling of. 4. Children of divorced parents—Counseling of. 5. Victims of family violence—Counseling of. 6. Group psychotherapy for children. 7. Children and violence.
  [DNLM: 1. Psychotherapy, Group—methods—Child. 2. Child Abuse—therapy. 3. Domestic Violence—psychology. 4. Family Therapy—methods. WS 350.2 S128 2005] I. Roseby, Vivienne, 1951-

RJ507.F33S34 2005
362.82'92—dc22

2005015892

CONTENTS

PART II: BIG KIDS' (BK) MANUAL

PART III: APPENDIXES

ABOUT THE AUTHORS

Vivienne Roseby, PhD, is a clinical psychologist in private practice and consultant to Families First Residential Treatment Center in Davis, California, with a specialty in a developmental understanding and treatment of children and adolescents with histories of acute and chronic trauma. She earned her PhD at the University of Wisconsin-Madison in the Department of Educational Psychology and has a double major in human development and school psychology and a double minor in clinical psychology and clinical social work. She has been a clinical consultant at the Child and Family Study Center at UC Davis.

Janet Johnston, PhD, is a sociologist, clinical social worker with a doctorate from Stanford University and a master's from the University of Michigan. She is currently professor in Justice Studies at the San Jose State University. Her specialty for the past two decades has been research and clinical interventions with high conflict and violent families, parental abduction of children, and alienated children. Dr. Johnston is co-author (with Dr. Roseby) of *In the Name of the Child: A Developmental Approach to Understanding and Helping Children of Conflicted and Violent Divorce,* as well as scores of other professional and scientific papers.

Bettina Gentner, LCSW, received her master's degree in social welfare from UC Berkeley with a specialty in direct services to families, children, and groups. She is formerly director of the children's program at Family Service Agency at San Mateo where she supervised scores of children's groups in socialization and trauma. She is now in private practice, consulting and teaching group intervention methods. She and Erin Moore have co-authored a group treatment manual called "Making and Keeping Friends."

Erin Moore, LCSW, received her master's in social work from the California State University at Hayward. She specializes in working in inpatient and outpatient treatment centers for traumatized children and adolescents.

All four authors have worked for Protecting Children from Conflict, an affiliate of the Judith Wallerstein Center for the Family in Transition in a special project designed to direct, implement, and evaluate group treatment services for children at-risk from family violence and abuse in local schools and neighborhood agencies in the San Francisco Bay Area.

Acknowledgments

This manual is the product of two decades of development and evaluation. The project was supported, in part, with funds from the Marin Community Foundation, the Van Loben Sels Foundation, and the Zellerbach Family Foundation. The evaluation of the program was funded by the David and Lucile Packard Foundation. We are especially grateful for the continued support of this project by the board of the Zellerbach Family Foundation and for the encouragement, insights, and guidance of its program officer, Ellen Walker, from 1996 through 2004, during the implementation phase in several San Francisco Bay Area counties.

Introduction

This manual presents a unique, step-by-step model for treating children who have experienced chronic conflict or violence within their families. The first edition was developed specifically for children of highly conflicted separating and divorced families who were referred by family courts to the Judith Wallerstein Center for the Family in Transition, which has been one of the country's foremost centers for divorce research.[1] The second edition includes changes that have been made to the model during the past seven years as it has been applied more broadly in multiethnic, multicultural neighborhoods, schools, and family agencies to help children who are living in a whole range of stressful situations related to family conflict and violence. Whereas the first edition focused solely on older school-age children, the second edition includes a section specifically designed for younger school-age children as well. Now the manual provides developmentally appropriate treatment curricula for children ranging from about five to fourteen years.

ABOUT THE PARTICIPANTS

We have learned that many children of chronically conflicted families tend to experience multiple stressful events. Many have lived with marital conflict and troubled or mentally ill parents or caretakers since birth. If the parents separate, the conflict and violence often do not resolve in such families, as parents remain bitterly and chronically embattled for years. In these fragile families, intact and separated, the children have to cope with an environment that is typified by their parents' distrust, anger, bitterness, blame, and fear of violence, and parenting that is unreliable, erratic, and at times frankly abusive.

The majority of children in conflicted families also have to cope with an unpredictable succession of parental partners and caretakers. Even when the children have at least one parenting adult who is an adequate or potentially "good enough" caretaker, he or she is typically overwhelmed with stresses related to poverty, social or cultural isolation, distance from supportive kin, lack of health care and employee benefits, long working hours, and low-paying jobs. These are children who are traumatized, often over the course of many years, by chronic exposure to frightening, fragmented, neglectful, and confusing relationships. Their emotional development is rarely sturdy.

Sadly, many children in the families whom we work with have to cope with not only chronic stress but also acute traumas that further impede and distort development. Witnessing domestic violence is the most frequently reported acute event. Excessive alcohol or drug use by parents or caretakers is common. About half of the children (and their siblings) have been directly physically abused and/or neglected. Some of them have been removed from their biological parents by the state and placed in the care of a grandparent, other relative, or foster home. Some children have experienced the police coming to their home, handcuffing a parent or older sibling, and taking him or her away. Others have experienced the incarceration of parents or other household members for family abuse or criminal behavior. Child abduction or the threat of abduction by a violent or emotionally disturbed parent is an additional acute trauma suffered by some of these children.

In a significant number of cases, inappropriate sexual behavior or molestation has been alleged or proven to have occurred. However, a word of caution: This treatment model does not purport to treat children who are primarily victims of sexual abuse. Other group treatment models are recommended for this specific purpose.[2] However, it is not unusual for children who have been sexually abused to disclose during their tenure in this treatment because of the co-occurrence of the sexual abuse trauma with other family abuse. They can benefit from this model before disclosure and after specific treatment for their sexual abuse.

HOW DO THESE CHILDREN PRESENT?

Surprisingly, these children are not always symptomatic nor obviously in need of help. In fact, some of them appear to be unusually resilient and mature. They are often nicely groomed. They may be quiet and apprehensive, but they can also appear lively and cheerful. It is easy to ignore their special challenges and hidden fragility, especially as many of them are so compliant and eager to please. Although some will manage to remain emotionally resilient, many, especially girls, will grow up depressed, anxious, insecure about themselves, and easily victimized by others. Without intervention, too many are smoldering time bombs, ready to explode during adolescence or young adulthood. They have the potential to wreak havoc in their families and our communities.

WHAT ARE THEIR CENTRAL CONCERNS AND HOW DO THEY AFFECT DEVELOPMENT?

When children are trying to survive and cope with their caretakers' conflict, violence, neediness, and unpredictability, they are, of necessity, preoccupied with special concerns, worries, and fears that we need to understand if we are to be helpful to them. It is our thesis that how these children try to manage their concerns has profound effects on their socioemotional development. These concerns include the following.

How Do I Keep Myself Safe?

Ordinarily, children develop their capacity to trust from the parents' relatively predictable responsiveness to their basic needs as infants. Later, as toddlers and young children, they rely on their parents to show them what is safe and trustworthy in the world. Children in high-conflict and violent families, however, face the paradox that the people who should provide them with love and protection are also the people who can be the most dangerous to them. They cannot trust their adults to be safe or to help them to know where safety lies. Consequently, these children have to provide for their own safety. Of necessity they devote most of their psychological energy to identifying where emotional or physical danger might be. Essentially, these children are always "combat ready": trained to filter out all signals of possible danger and ignore nonthreatening information that is essentially irrelevant to their safety. They are preoccupied with questions about who is safe, who is dangerous, who can be trusted, and what is predictable.

These questions about trust, safety, and predictability are expressed in play therapy when these children reveal worlds in which characters turn capriciously from evil witches into good fairies, tame animals turn wild, and allies become enemies. One four-year-old boy's sand-tray play captured the predicament. He placed a small child doll (himself) in the center of a battlefield and commented, "But the good people wore bad masks and the bad people wore good masks. I wasn't sure which to follow." Some children manage their confusion about parents who are loving and then unpredictably moody or violent by holding a "double image" of that parent. A ten-year-old boy, for example, had a recurring dream of identical twin fathers ("men who looked like my dad, but didn't") in which one of the fathers tried to protect him from the sadistic violence of the other.

Developmental Consequences

Psychological testing indicates that these children, as a group, are likely to be hypervigilant and mistrusting of others.[3] They view the world as an uncooperative place and maintain a watchful, guarded stance from which they are ever scanning for dangers. In extreme cases these children develop a paranoid and hostile worldview. For them the enduring dilemma is that they do not feel safe until they have found danger. Because they believe that danger (physical or emotional) is always present, the children either correctly identify a danger or distort a benign situation as simply masking a hidden danger. Paradoxically, the identification (however distorted) keeps anxiety at bay. Not surprisingly these hypervigilant children do not turn to others for guidance or interpretation of the world as typically developing children are able to do. Instead, they become introversive, turning to themselves as their own best resource. They are so preoccupied with maintaining control and distance that they cannot accept empathy, direction, or support.

How Do I Figure Out What Is True and What Is Real?

These children chronically struggle with the puzzle of parents' and other adults' conflicting claims about what is true and what is not. Their particular worries vary with age and cognitive stage. For example a four-year-old worried, "Is Daddy's new girlfriend really a witch?" The reality concerns of a nine-year-old tend to be less magical, but no less troubling. For example, "Dad made Mom have an abortion—does that mean he made her kill my little brother?"

Some children have feelings of loyalty or fear toward a parent that distort their understanding of what is real and what is true. For example, a five-year-old stated, "My dad broke . . . no, no, my mother made my dad break her wrist!" Children's perceptions about a parent's dangerousness can become confused with their own fears and destructive wishes and reflect little of what is actually real. An eight-year-old boy, for example, described how he watched his parents' physical struggle as he "prayed and prayed to God to stop Mom killing my dad." In actuality, the father was abusive to the children, and the mother had thrown herself at the father in order to protect them. The boy was furious with his father for abusing him, but he was too afraid of his own murderous impulses to acknowledge them as his own. By projecting his anger onto his mother this boy had safe access to the anger, but his understanding of reality was powerfully distorted.

Developmental Consequences

The overwhelming majority of these children have significantly unusual or frankly distorted perceptions of the interpersonal world. Moreover, given the distrust and introversion that typifies this population, these distorted perceptions are unlikely to be changed by ordinary communication with others. As a result, these children are using a distorted and entrenched understanding of reality as their absolute reference for understanding themselves, other people, and relationships.

How Do I Keep Life Predictable?

Children who are traumatized within their families typically experience their relationships as unpredictable and double binding. The result is an overwhelming sense of confusion that they try to control by dismissing perceptions, ideas, or demands that are ambiguous, subtle, or complex. They limit themselves instead to a narrow and simplified perceptual field so that their information, ideas, and conclusions remain simple, predictable, concrete, and utilitarian. This kind of psychological tunnel vision is illustrated by children who blandly state, "Dad is right, he's perfectly cool! Mom is wrong, bad!" Friends who meet a need are "nice and good," and friends who do not meet a need are easily dismissed as "mean and bad." The children's ideas about themselves remain equally undeveloped and tend to swing between an unrealistic sense of perfect goodness and an equally unrealistic sense of absolute badness.

Developmental Consequences

Many of these children develop a highly constricted and oversimplified cognitive style to keep the unpredictability of their world from becoming overwhelming. Their almost phobic avoidance of nuance and complexity naturally limits the development of their social maturity and interpersonal understanding. The children's moral development is also compromised because they are rarely raised according to an objective and reliable moral code of right and wrong. Instead, ideas of right and wrong tend to be defined in a highly personal way by the changing needs of unpredictable parents or caretakers. What is right becomes whatever meets the parent's need and keeps the child safe, and what is wrong is what does not meet the parent's need and, as a result, leaves the child unsafe. In other relationships, the children's highly oversimplified or distorted cognitive style leads them to view people who meet their needs as "good" and those who do not as "bad."

How Do I Stop the Fighting?

Children in violent and conflicted families tend to believe that they are responsible for the fighting. Although this conviction is an impossible burden, it is also a defense against feeling helpless in the face of chaotic events and relationships. The younger ones believe they cause the fight or that they have the power to control it. A five-year-old girl, for example, decided that she was magic, " 'Cause when I come in the room they stop fighting." Older children tend to feel greater self-blame. As one twelve-year-old boy said, "If I were dead they wouldn't need to fight anymore." Age and experience have taught him that there is no magic, only a sense of responsibility that makes the helplessness more shameful and more difficult to bear.

Developmental Consequences

Although these children often present themselves as competent or even pseudomature, it should not be surprising that testing shows significant vulnerability in their self-esteem and sense of effectiveness and competence in the world. Their self-importance in relation to others is vastly diminished. Test results and play also reveal the brutal effect of their perceived failure to stop their parents' fighting and violence; the children see themselves as bad, damaged, nonviable, and inadequate. These effects stand in stark contrast to the experience of typically developing children, who are free to be self-focused, ensuring that their own needs are met and allowing them to take pleasure in their developing competencies.

How Do I Keep My Parents Safe?

In the presence of constant anger and threat of violence, and in response to the profound neediness of distressed parents, children become urgently concerned about the emotional and physical well-being of their primary caretakers. A child as young as four may worry that his or her mother will be "sad and cry if she is on her own." A ten-year-old boy monitored his depressed, alcoholic father's state constantly. "I know how to get him out of his sad moods. I just do something wrong, and then he gets mad and he yells. Then he's not sad anymore." The children's caretaking of the parent is also an attempt to manage their own fears of loss and abandonment. Holding on to and preventing the loss of the parent or caregiver is often a much more central concern than the violence itself. We were reminded of this by an eleven-year-girl whom we had taken into therapy when her parents separated in chaos. The father had been consistently violent and accused the mother of drug use and unfaithfulness. At eleven, the girl seemed unwilling or unable to talk about her father's violence in her therapy. When she was seventeen, her teacher sent us an essay that was essentially a poignant letter to her mother. The letter revealed not fear of her abusive father, but desolate loneliness at age eleven when her mother went out at night and terror that her mother would die from taking drugs.

Developmental Consequences

In order to attend and respond to the adults' emotional state, these children ignore or dismiss their own needs and feelings. Psychological testing confirms the pervasive emotional constriction that results when children inhibit the natural exuberance of childhood in order to focus on their caretaker's well-being.[4] It is not only liveliness that is flattened here, but aggression as well. Instead the children are likely to maintain a covertly negative, alienated, and oppositional stance that is masked by an apparent eagerness to please. This surface tends to disintegrate in the face of intense stress and then regression, irritability, or violent behavior may occur.

A SUMMARY PROFILE OF CHILDREN WHO LIVE WITH CONFLICT AND VIOLENCE

These children live with particular preoccupations, fears, and concerns that affect every aspect of how they think and feel about the interpersonal world. While appearing to be competent and even mature, they are, in actuality, profoundly guarded and mistrusting. They learn to see themselves as their own best resource, vigilantly focused on the needs of others and determined to achieve and maintain maximum predictability and control. Sadly, what they are most able to control are their own thoughts, feelings, and perceptions of reality. Their exercise of this control leaves them emotionally and cognitively constricted and avoidant of new experiences that would lead to growth. As a result, these children develop few inner resources or external sources of support. The bind is that they nevertheless turn to their own impoverished inner world to make sense of and manage their lives. Their rules of behavior are often harsh and lacking in nuance, their capacity for empathy compromised by "black and white" thinking. Not surprisingly, these limited resources tend to become overwhelmed by situational demands, so that the children often feel inadequate, helpless, and alienated. As adolescents, they struggle with an incoherent sense of self, have difficulty authoring a coherent narrative of their past, and dare not hope or dream for a better future.

LONG-TERM EFFECTS

As we have noted, these children do organize themselves to cope, though most of their coping strategies are unconscious. Their efforts focus primarily on maximizing predictability and control in a chaotic world. Over time the unconscious exercise of these coping strategies shape rigid scripts, or blueprints for understanding themselves, other people, and relationships. Although each child's script is uniquely shaped by particular experience, the goal is always to maximize a sense of predictability, safety, and control. These unconscious scripts are often the most stable and reliable organizers that the child has. They provide the only available short-term safety. Over the long term, however, the scripts become the foundation for an inflexible way of thinking, feeling, and relating to people that often carries the imprint of violence or victimization as the norm of intimacy. As adults they are at increased risk for developing personality disorders and/or becoming violent or victimized in their own relationships. The need for intervention is serious and clear; however, the children's dedication to control makes them difficult to redirect. They are typically so mistrustful and controlling that they are extremely difficult to engage in individual counseling or psychotherapy.

WHAT ARE THE GOALS OF THIS GROUP APPROACH?

The overall goal of this model is to help the children bring their internal scripts to the surface and challenge the rules and expectations that support them. As the children's internal scripts are deconstructed, new thoughts, feelings, and ideas can be experienced in the context of group interaction. Although we recognize that no single group can provide enough change to reverse long-term effects, we do know that carefully structured activities can help authentic and spontaneous new experiences find their way under these children's barriers. When this happens, children tend to be compelled by and attracted to the possibilities that exist beyond the constricted scripts of their worlds. They begin to know about other ways of being. These internal shifts can propel children toward a different and healthier developmental trajectory.

This overall goal is accomplished by addressing specific developmental threats that are the foundation of children's scripts. We address these threats in a theoretically coherent, cost-effective, and practical way. Although these strategies have been developed primarily for groups, many of the activities can also be adapted for use in individual work, most particularly for children who need a greater degree of structure in the early or more difficult stages of treatment. The specific developmental threats observed in these children and corresponding therapeutic goals are as follows:

Developmental Deficits	Therapeutic Goals
1. Hypervigilance, distrust, and tendency to rely upon self as only help resource when solving problems	1. *Create common ground and safety,* and pleasurable opportunities to use peers to resolve interpersonal problems
2. Constriction of feelings, difficulty modulating affect and tolerating ambivalence	2. *Explore the language and complexity of feelings,* which helps express and mediate between inner experience and observable behavior
3. Low egocentricity and self-efficacy, poor interpersonal boundaries	3. *Defining and understanding the self,* differentiating one's own from others' feelings, ideas, and preferences, and, hence, empowering self
4. Overly simplified, rigid, and distorted views of people and relationships	4. *Defining and revising roles and relationships,* exploring nuance and complexity, tolerating ambiguity
5. Harsh, rigid rules of conduct condemning self or others; violator-versus-victim stance; disillusioned, failure to hope and dream	5. *Restoring a moral order* that is compassionate and supports healthy idealism and hope for one's future

THE ACTIVITIES AND OVERALL TREATMENT PLAN

What Activities Are Used and How Are They Related to the Therapeutic Goals?

The sequence of activities within the group model is summarized according to each of the five goals as follows. The activities or exercises, though structured, are designed to evoke content relevant to the unique needs and concerns of the participants. That is, it is not assumed that specific stressful life events such as divorce or witnessing domestic violence are the central defining event or an immediate concern. Rather, in drawing, group discussion, and dramatization, the children's own worries, fears, and preoccupations are surfaced. This balance of providing a structured therapeutic curriculum that generates content unique to each child and group represents a middle ground between a psychoeducational (or cookbook) approach, which can limit the leader's ability to respond to the unique needs and histories of each group member, and an unstructured process group, which would not necessarily address the developmental deficits in any useful way. The specific group exercises that address each of the five goals are summarized in the following.

Creating Common Ground and Safety

The group should be a safe place where the children can learn from and about their peers. This is especially important for youngsters who tend to control and avoid rather than form real relationships.

Rules (BK Session 1,C; LK Session 1,C). Children create a brief list of rules for safe conduct within the group. It is posted in the group room during every session.

Family drawing (BK Session 1,D; LK Session 2,D). Children are asked to draw their families. In this activity they can find common ground as well as support for the many different forms of family.

Blind walk (BK Session 2,B). Each blind walker (a group member who is selected or who volunteers) is blindfolded and led through an obstacle course that the other group members create especially for him or her. The activity builds unity and trust among the children as they help one another to find their way in the face of unknown dangers.

Relaxation (BK Sessions 3,B-8,C; LK Sessions 4,B-11,B). The leader guides the children through a progressive relaxation exercise. This helps the children to become aware of their feeling states and provides a way to ease their physical tensions.

Group art project (BK Session 9,C). Children work together without words to build a statue using a variety of common objects such as macaroni, straws, fabric scraps, and so on. The leader emphasizes the value of peer support and cooperation.

Exploring the Language and Complexity of Feelings

Many children in conflicted families have little experience using language to express their own emotions. In part this is because feelings often seem frightening and uncontrollable. Acknowledging feelings out loud can make them seem terrifyingly personal and real. This causes a significant bind because children need words in order to share their experiences with other people. Feeling words also provide an alternative to acting out feelings. This is a step that many of the children have neither practiced nor witnessed. It is important to create an environment in which the expression of feelings is not only permitted and encouraged, but especially valued.

List of feelings (BK Session 1,E; LK Sessions 1,D and 3,B). The children brainstorm a list of feelings or feeling faces. The list is posted in the group room for reference in every session.

Color feelings (BK Session 1,F). With a primary color, the children underline each basic feeling on the feeling chart. They then combine primary colors for more complex emotions. This allows the children to use colors as well as feeling words to communicate about feelings. The activity also introduces the group to the idea of blended feelings. This idea is crucial for children whose thoughts, feelings, and ideas about people and relationships tend to be oversimplified.

Level of feeling (BK Session 2,C; LK Sessions 4,C and 5,C). The children complete a chart with six empty thermometers (or feeling faces) that can be filled in with color to show levels of feeling. The activity introduces the idea that feelings have different levels of intensity.

Charade of feeling (BK Session 2,D; LK Sessions 3,C and 4,E). Each child charades a feeling from their levels of feeling chart (or feeling faces). The group's task is to guess the feeling as well as the level of that feeling. The leader uses questions and discussion to help the children to understand that feelings and actions are different and that feelings cannot be controlled or judged, but actions can. It is in the domain of action that children can begin to consider the question of what is right and wrong behavior in a relationship.

Inside me/outside me (BK Session 7,D). Children use two sheets of paper, stapled together, with an identical outline of a human figure on each sheet. The children color the top figure with colors of the feelings they show and the bottom figure with the feelings they keep inside. The activity helps children to understand that they do not have to control their feelings and ideas quite so much if they can control how they express them to other people.

Masks (BK Session 7,E; LK Session 11,D,E). Children create masks to represent the self that they show to the world. In role-plays the children put the masks on when they need them for safety and remove them when they feel safe to share their true feelings. In the LK group this exercise is done with a puppet play using Koko and Bunny.

Defining and Understanding the Self

Children in high-conflict families tend to find safety in responding to the needs and expectations of other people. They often lose sight of their own feelings, ideas, motives, and preferences in the process. Children are vulnerable to losing a secure sense of themselves in relationships when they are primed to give in to others in this way. Young children have particular difficulty experiencing themselves as constant and cohesive and are prone to splitting their feelings and views of self and other into dichotomies of bad/good and feeling/nonfeeling (experiencing their own feelings is interpreted by the children as bad because their feelings may conflict with what they perceive it is that others want; nonfeeling is good because it allows them to more easily fulfill the expectations of others since their own desires will not get in the way).

Koko and Bunny puppet plays (LK Sessions 5-11). Two group members, Koko (a gorilla with big, wild, and often uncontrollable feelings) and Bunny (a constricted white rabbit who tends to suffer somatic symptoms), act out a series of skits, some of which are taken from the book *Where the Wild Things Are*. The children identify with both puppets, and with the help of Max/Maxine (the integrator), also a puppet, they help the puppets gradually learn to accept and modulate both extremes of feeling and being. See page 88 for information regarding the use of the puppets.

"Who's there?" (LK Session 6,C) and *"One thing I will always remember about you"* (LK Session 12,E). These two exercises teach young children that they are kept in mind when out of sight of others who care about them.

Points of view (BK Session 2,E). Pairs of children role-play an argument between parents about a box (made by the leader according to instructions in the manual) that is black on one side, white on the other, and black, white, and gray on the ends. Each of the "parents" is positioned on either side of the box so that only the black or white is visible. One argues that the box is white, the other argues that the box is black. Those watching are the "children." They are positioned to see the ends of the box that are black, white, and also gray. The activity introduces the children to the idea that other perspectives about their parents' conflict are possible.

A fantasy room (BK Session 3,C). Children are invited to imagine and then draw a private room that no one else can enter without their permission. The room may be any size, shape, color, or location and may contain whatever the child wishes. The room is a way to represent the self. The walls represent a boundary between the self and others. In subsequent sessions the leader has the option of using guided imagery to help the children enter this inner space in their minds. It becomes a safe place of retreat, where children can identify private thoughts, feelings, or wishes.

The gift (BK Session 4,C). The leader guides the children to their "inner room" and suggests that they find a gift there. Once the image is in place, the leader asks them to think about what the gift is, who sent it, and whether there is a message attached. Once the children have identified their gift, they can draw a picture of it in their room. This addition, like others that follow, becomes a concrete way of representing the children's expanding sense of self.

The private wish (BK Session 5,C). The leader guides the children to their "inner room" and suggests that they find a blackboard there. Once there, they are to imagine that they write down a private wish on the blackboard. The wish is then written on paper, placed inside an envelope, and taped to the drawing of the imaginary room.

The mirror (BK Session 6,C). The children imagine looking into a mirror in their imaginary room. They are asked to notice what they like and do not like about themselves, as well as anything they wish to change now or as they get older. Children can tape their list of written responses to the drawing of the imaginary room.

The statue (BK Session 7,C). The children are guided to their imaginary rooms to imagine a statue of how they really feel inside. They also imagine what the statue might do if it came to life. This activity introduces the idea of an inner self and an outer self.

Keys to the room (BK Session 8,C1). The children are introduced to the idea that they can use their "private rooms" as a retreat when they are not in the group any longer. In this activity, they practice going to the room in their minds and then leaving it again.

A wish for tomorrow (BK Session 8, C2-3). The children are asked to think about themselves as they might be when they are adults and to make a wish for themselves at that age. The wish is written on a piece of paper shaped like an apple seed and "planted" in a paper cup. The cup is taped closed with instructions not to open it until the year that each individual child becomes an adult.

Letter to parents (BK Session 8,F; LK Session 12,D). The children work as a group to write a joint letter to all of the parents. The content addresses "things that I want you to know about me." All the children sign the letter, which becomes group property.

Identity shields (BK Session 10,D1). The identity shield helps the children to consider the kind of person they want to become as they move toward adolescence. The children each receive a poster board with a shield shape that is divided into five sections: two for parents, two for important others, and one for the child. They write or draw symbols of the qualities in each person that they admire and wish to keep as part of their shield. They also draw or write the qualities they reject on the outside of the appropriate section. Finally, the shield shape is cut from the poster board and the rejected qualities fall away. The shield represents an ideal, or moral compass, that can guide the children as they mature.

Defining and Revising Roles and Relationships

When children role-play their own and other people's parts in a remembered situation, they bring perceptions, thoughts, and feelings (that have shaped their ideas about relationships) back into aware-ness. When perceptions, thoughts, and feelings are made conscious in this way, they can be available for revision.

Rules of role-play (BK Session 3,D). The leader prompts role-plays with a series of pictures (included in the manual) that suggest situations that are common in high-conflict families. When these pictures are not relevant, the leader may substitute others or simply allow the children to suggest their own situations. The child who volunteers the role-play situation may direct the group members, telling them what feelings, thoughts, and actions go with their individual roles. After each role-play, the leader asks the director to develop a revised version that shows how he or she wishes the situation had gone. All of the role-plays are videotaped by a designated group member. The children review and discuss the videotapes at the end of each session. Directing, role-playing, role-switching, revising, and video review-ing all provide opportunities for the children to surface and recon-sider thoughts and feelings about the reenacted event. In so doing, they gain a measure of distance and mastery.

Role-play of child caught between parents (BK Session 3,E) and *Bunny, Koko, and conflict* (LK Session 9,C,D). These dramatizations evoke children's thoughts and feelings about their role in their parents' conflicts and how to cope.

Role-play of child going between houses (BK Session 4,D; LK Session 8,C,D). This role-play can capture children's thoughts and feelings about going back and forth between their parents. The transi-tions may refer to visits between different homes or within the zone of conflict in the same home.

Masks and role-plays (BK Session 7,E). Children role-play situa-tions in which they had to hide their real feelings. In the role-play they use the masks that they have created when they are hiding their feel-ings. At certain points in the role-play they remove the masks to tell the camera what they really feel underneath. The leader helps the children to consider when and with whom they feel safe enough to re-move their masks.

Family sculpture (BK Session 8,D). The leader helps each group member to form the other group members into a human sculpture of his or her family. The sculpture represents the child's view of the way people in his or her family relate to each other most of the time. When the sculpture is completed, it is silently videotaped. The leader then helps each child to identify the ways that the sculpture shows his or her ideas about what is expected in family relationships.

The Turtle Story (BK Session 10,C). The leader reads a story about a sea turtle and a land turtle who loved each other and had sea-land turtle children together. Eventually, though, the adult turtles were so different that it was impossible for them to be happy together. The story provides a way for the children to understand their parents' conflict in a reasonable, nonblaming way. The story also introduces the possibility that being a child of two very different people can be an asset rather than a liability.

Turtle Story role-plays (BK Session 10,D2). The children reenact The Turtle Story (BK Session 10,C), explaining why parents had to separate and divorce and creating their own versions in the process.

Restoring a Moral Order

Children who live with conflict tend to develop rigid and sometimes distorted ideas about family roles, relationships, and morality. Activities that address these issues are designed to raise questions about what is right, fair, and expectable in relationships, as well as to surface feelings that are associated with these concerns.

Jobs for people in your family (BK Session 5,D). The leader helps the children to define areas of responsibility that are appropriate for children (e.g., learning in school, following the rules) and those that are appropriate for adults (e.g., protecting the children, settling their own fights).

Review of rules (BK Session 5,F1; for older children). The older children clarify rules of moral conduct as they review the videotape of the role-plays about right and wrong that are conducted in BK Session 5.

Review of jobs (BK Session 5,F2; for younger children). In the review of the videotape of the role-plays about right and wrong in session 5, the younger children clarify whether the jobs that the role-players have taken on are appropriate for them.

Role-plays about right and wrong (BK Session 5,E) and *Bunny and Koko have a fight* (LK Session 7,D). These role-plays are often developed in response to a picture of a child watching parents who are fighting. The leader uses the role-plays and the revised versions to help the children to consider their thoughts and feelings about right and wrong ways for people to treat one another in relationships.

Role-plays of feelings and actions (BK Session 6,E; LK Session 10,C,D,E). Children (or the puppets) role-play situations in which they or another person had very strong feelings and acted on them in a wrong or unhelpful way. The children create revised role-plays to practice alternative methods of conflict resolution.

How to act on feelings (BK Session 6,D). The leader helps the children to identify right and wrong ways to act on feelings.

Role-plays and facts about feelings and actions (BK Session 6,E). The leader provides five facts about the differences between feelings and actions.

Fantasy family sculpture (BK Session 8,E). Each child creates an ideal version of his or her family sculpture. It is silently videotaped. The sculpture of the ideal family provides the children with an opportunity to review and revise their ideas about relationships and their own role in the family. This second part of the exercise can evoke very strong feelings, so the work requires careful monitoring by the leader at every step.

TV panel of experts (BK Session 9,D1; for older children). Children create a panel of experts about family conflict and divorce. The panel is dramatized and videotaped as a television talk show. Members of the panel give advice to children living with conflict, who send "questions" (prepared by the leader according to the instructions in the manual) to the panel. The activity helps the children to clarify and confirm their own ideas about relationships.

Solving dilemmas (BK Session 9,D2; for younger children). Children role-play dilemmas and work together to identify different ways of coping with or solving them.

Why Is a Group Model a Good Idea?

In the authors' experience, children who have lived with conflict show a marked preference for group over individual treatment. In group they can reduce some of the shame about their family situation and find out that they are "not the only one." The group also provides a developmentally appropriate opportunity for school-age children to learn from and about their peers in activities rather than in conversation. Parents also seem to tolerate the suggestion that their child participate in group better than a suggestion for individual therapy. Group therapy reassures parents that their child is more normal, and similar to other kids; and they do not feel that they are being replaced by a therapist who can parent their child better than they can.

Is There a Group Model for Parents?

Children gain maximum benefit from participating in this group approach when their parents are actively working to manage or reduce their conflict and to understand and protect their children more effectively. This work is best conducted by the clinician who is leading the children's group; it is the leader's direct experience of the child in the group that underscores his or her credibility to the parents and heightens their awareness and motivation. Work with parents can be conducted individually (in conjoint or separate sessions) or in psychoeducational groups, which may be scheduled during the same ten- to twelve-week period as the children's meetings and can be a cost-effective and efficient approach to the kind of collateral work with parents that best supports the children. The structure and content of psychoeducational groups for parents are described in Appendix B of this manual.

Does Any Research Support the Effectiveness of This Approach?

Yes! See the study by J. R. Johnston (2003), "Group Interventions for Children at Risk from Abuse and Witness to Violence: A Report of a Study," in the *Journal of Emotional Abuse,* Vol. 3, pp. 203-226. A brief report of the findings appears in Appendix C.

ABOUT THE LEADERS

What Qualifications Should the Leader Have, and How Many Leaders Should There Be?

This group approach requires at least one leader who is a trained mental health professional with experience working with children both individually and in groups. This person must also be experienced in working with parents in groups, individually, and in marriage and divorce counseling. The decision to use one or two group leaders depends upon the availability of resources, the training and experience of the leaders, and the specific needs of the children in the group. One leader with a good deal of experience may be successful, particularly with more mature groups. In general, however, coleadership is recommended. Two leaders can manage acting-out behavior more effectively. Discussions between the coleaders can also provide the children with a model of conflict resolution that they have not observed before. Although at least one of the coleaders should be an experienced clinician, the other may be in training or a paraprofessional.

PLANNING AND MANAGING A GROUP

How Should I Prepare to Lead a Group?

We recommend a thorough reading of the entire manual before proceeding. A careful review will provide a framework for using the manual responsibly and effectively. We draw particular attention to the previous section, The Activities and Overall Treatment Plan, where we provide an overview of the sequence of activities, the therapeutic goals they address, and the sessions in which they appear. This overview can help the leader to tailor the pacing of activities as well as to decide which can be omitted due to lack of time or relevance.

What Kind of Intake and Screening Information Do I Need?

The group leader should meet individually with each child prior to accepting the child into the group. The group leader will also need to know as much about the child's family history as possible before including the child in the group. It will be important to know, for example, how long the parents have been in conflict and whether the child has witnessed violence (how much and at what age). This information may come from interviews with parents (conducted by phone or in person) or written questionnaires. The more details the leader has, the more he or she will be able to prompt and support each child in the group. It will also be important for the leader to know how the child has coped with group situations in the past. This can be evaluated by means of interviews with teachers and parents. Behavior checklists can be used as well. Children who have a history of acting out (which can be difficult to manage in group settings) may not be appropriate for group treatment unless sufficient staffing support can be made available.

How Many Children Should Be in Each Group?

The groups should range in size from no less than five to no more than eight participants. Optimally, they should include a balance of boys and girls. When this gender balance is not possible, the leader has to consider what mix of gender and personalities might maximize the children's sense of safety.

Should I Include Siblings in the Same Group?

When siblings fall into the same age range the decision to include them in one group rests with the leader and his or her intake information about the family. In some cases, siblings bring comfort and support to each other in the course of the group experience. In other cases, children may have taken sides against each other in the family conflict, or one child may be overshadowed by the other. In these situations it is preferable for each child to have a separate group experience. It is not unusual for siblings to warn each other not to share family secrets when both are part of the same group. This will alert the leader to possible issues that need to be discussed with parents so that children can be given permission to freely disclose their concerns in group.

What Is the Age Range for Children in Groups?

We recommend the therapeutic curriculum described in Part I of this manual for the youngest children (five to six years) and Part II for older children, separated roughly into the following age groups: seven to nine years; ten to twelve years; and thirteen to fourteen years. Note that many of the group activities in Part II are specifically labeled as suitable for younger children only, and others are labeled as suitable for the older age groups.

Older children (ages ten to fourteen) meet for ninety-minute sessions, younger children (ages five to nine) generally meet for one hour. Separating groups according to age ranges allows the leaders to tailor each group's tempo, activity, and discussion to their particular developmental capacities.

How Should I Prepare for Each Session?

Once the group is underway, it is important for the leader to review the session plans before each meeting and to have a general idea about which activities might be emphasized and which might be minimized or dropped entirely. This judgment will be based upon the leader's ability to match the needs of a particular group to the therapeutic goal of the activity. The needs of a particular group can be determined by intake procedures and ongoing experience with the children in session. The therapeutic goal of the activity can be determined by reading the clinical notes within each session. These clinical notes explain the connection between the activity and the therapeutic goal.

Can I Change the Wording of the Instructions to the Children in Each Session?

Yes! The words in the manual are suggestions to help the leader be completely clear about the nature of the activity. It is important, however, for the leader to read the manual and then to translate the words to fit the way that he or she naturally talks to the children. If this translating does not happen, the group experience will seem stilted and unnatural.

Do I Have to Include All of the Activities in Every Session?

No! In most sessions there will be more activities than time allows. In addition, some activities will generate a lot of discussion and interest, while others will not. The leader will need to have an idea about which activities seem most relevant, as well as their place in the whole sequence of the group approach. With these considerations in mind, the leader can decide what to spend time on and what to drop.

What if the Children Are Acting Out?

Refer to Appendix A on troubleshooting at the end of this manual.

Do I Have to Give Snack?

Snack is one way to help these children to feel nurtured and safe. Snack works best when the food is not brought to the room until it is snack time and when it is available in unlimited quantities (i.e., popcorn) or in specified quantities (i.e., two cookies each, no more).

What if Ten to Twelve Sessions Are Not Enough?

For some children, particularly those in the general divorcing population, the group treatment plus additional work with parents will provide adequate support. Others benefit from being able to participate in more than ten sessions. Leaders may decide to extend the number of sessions because each session in this manual details a very full agenda; all together, there is enough material for twenty or more sessions. Some leaders have evolved ongoing groups that periodically graduate old members and admit new ones. Some children benefit from cycling through two or three different ten-session groups. Finally, some children are more able to feel comfortable in individual counseling after their experience in group treatment.

How Can I Get a Better Understanding of the Treatment Needs of These Children?

For a more complete discussion of children who live in highly conflicted or violent families as well as the theoretical rationale for this treatment approach, we recommend the companion volume to this manual—*In the Name of the Child: A Developmental Approach to Understanding and Helping Children of Conflicted and Violent Divorce* (Johnston and Roseby, 1997, New York: The Free Press).

ADAPTING THE GROUP TO CULTURAL/ETHNIC DIFFERENCES

These groups have been implemented within Caucasian, Hispanic, Asian, and African-American communities. They have been conducted primarily in English and Spanish and occasionally in both languages concurrently. To ensure adaptation within these different contexts it is most important to have competent bicultural and bilingual group leaders who are also flexible and skilled clinicians. When minority cultures are particularly sensitive about family privacy, fear exposure about family problems, and are uncomfortable about mental health referrals it is important to embed the children's group program within neighborhood centers and local schools that provide a broad array of educational, employment, and health services. In these settings, family advocates who are indigenous to the community are valuable team members who work closely with the group leaders and can outreach to the family, assist with referrals to the group, and help provide feedback to parents and other caregivers. Other adaptations are as follows:

- Children from disadvantaged social classes and minority communities often have a different sense of family. It is important for the group leaders to change the language about families to include a wide range of types and relationships. Aunts, uncles, grandparents, older siblings, foster parents, and family friends may be their primary caregivers, and multiple families may be living in their homes.
- Children in these families, especially the older ones, may assume unusually heavy responsibilities for caring for their siblings, provisioning, cooking, and house cleaning. They may even contribute to the economic support of their family. Clinicians need to be careful in concluding that these are necessarily inappropriate or pathological role-reversals between parents and children.
- In many of the more traditional cultures, parents do not necessarily ask children what they think or feel about things, and "back talk" is unacceptable. They may subscribe to the philosophy that "children should be seen and not heard." For these reasons their children may have had little experience identifying

and talking about feelings. Hence, more time and attention needs to be given to the development of a language of feelings, when and where to safely express their ideas, and especially how to manage negative feelings such as anxiety, sadness, and anger.

- We have found that children of different cultural and family backgrounds vary in the manner in which they release tension and calm themselves. Whereas the quiet, deep-breathing exercises that are described in this manual are comfortable methods for some, others seem to become anxious and fidgety at such times. Instead, these children might benefit from brisk physical exercise, belly-shaking laughter, and other intense, fun activities.

- Children from divorced families disputing custody are often imbued with a heightened sense of being "special" and central to the emotional survival of their parents. In other cases, children in large families troubled by substance abuse and domestic violence may feel stigmatized and unimportant. In the first case, children can have defensively high self-esteem, and in the second case they may suffer low self-esteem. Paradoxically, in both situations children feel anxious and vulnerable. The group leader needs to use language that helps each child feel *appropriately competent and valued* without implying demands to be special or different in ways that would make them feel uncomfortable or burdened.

- Children for whom English is their second language tend to be less proficient and comfortable with the more cognitive-verbal exercises described in this manual. They have no difficulty, however, in expressing themselves in mime and acting in role-plays. Group leaders may also need to adapt the projective exercises to different mediums. Specifically, in some Asian cultures storytelling is an age-old tradition for transmitting values, rituals, and morals. For African Americans music, dance, and drama may be more comfortable mediums for communicating these ideas. Children of all cultures usually enjoy stories with characters they can identify with and act out. A list of therapeutic stories for children exposed to different kinds of stressful and traumatic situations is provided in the bibliography of this manual for these purposes.

PART I:
LITTLE KIDS' (LK) MANUAL

Saying Hello and Making Me Feel Safe in Group

Goals

To create a sense of safety and privacy
To create group cohesion
To create a sense of shared history

Materials

Bunny and Koko puppets[1]
Thick paper for name tags
Manila file folders
Two large pieces of paper, taped to the wall
Lots of paper, markers, and pencils

Procedure

A. Introduction

Each week, when the children arrive, they are asked to sit in a circle. This is the format for the beginning (and ending) of each week's group, though many of the activities require a less formal approach. The leaders introduce themselves and discuss the purpose of the group. It can be interesting to ask the children if they know, or if someone explained to them, why they have come today. The group leader can say:

We are all together today because everyone here has had some difficult things happen in their families. Some children have seen adults fighting or not being nice to each other. Some children have families where people aren't safe or do things that are scary for children. In some families, children have a mom and a dad who don't live with each other.

It is important to allow the children in the group some time to respond to the leader's statements. A few of them may want to share their experiences or events that have occurred in their families; some may not. Although the leader can ask a child, "Would you like to say something?" no one should be forced to share if he or she is not ready.

After each child says his or her name, Koko and Bunny are introduced to the group:

> We would like to introduce you to two other group members. This is Bunny. This is Koko. Bunny and Koko are just like everybody else in the group because sometimes they feel scared, sometimes they feel mad, and sometimes they feel happy. They feel like they are in the middle of all their family problems, too.

The children in the group may want to touch the puppets or ask Bunny and Koko some questions about their feelings or family. Remember, they are not to wear them. (Please see page 90 for clinical rationale.)

B. Folders and Name Tags

Each child is given a piece of paper to make a name tag. File folders cut up into four pieces are good sizes for name tags. These name tags are kept by the group leaders and put out each week whether or not the child attends that week. This is a way that each child is remembered, even if she or he is not in the group for that week's session.

Instead of or in addition to these name tags, the children can each be given a blank manila file folder. The leaders explain to the group that their drawings and artwork will be kept in these folders and returned to them at the last group.

The children can decorate these while the group continues. Some young children may request help spelling or writing their names. Each child is asked to work on her or his own name tag or folder to encourage self-responsibility. Doing the work for their peers is definitely discouraged. The group leaders may want to make name tags for Bunny and Koko if the children in the group suggest or request it, but it is not necessary.

Clinical note: Some children want to take their artwork home each time. Preventing them from doing this frees the children from the burden of having to give gifts or trying to please their parents or guardians. It also maintains the children's confidentiality.

C. Group Rules

A large sheet of paper is taped to the wall and titled GROUP RULES. The children are asked to suggest rules for this list. Staff may say, "Let's think of some rules for our group that will help us all feel safe." One of the leaders writes the children's suggestions on the paper. Bunny and Koko help the children generate ideas for this list, but the majority of the ideas should come from the group members.

It is important that the rules of confidentiality are included. A group leader can say:

> Whatever we talk about in group is private. We don't tell your parents/grown-ups what we do or say in this room because it's private. We only tell them things if someone is in danger or going to get hurt. So, whatever is said in here stays in here. You can tell your parents/grown-ups what you did or said, but please don't tell them what other children did or said.

If the children are having some difficulty coming up with rules, especially regarding safety, Koko or Bunny could say to the children:

> Hey, I have rules in my classroom. They are like these rules, but we have some at school that aren't on our list. What are they? Oh gosh, I can't remember. What rules do you have in your classroom?

Clinical note: For this and other lists the group generates, it is important for the staff to be the "secretary" for the group and do the writing. The children will offer, as they try to please the adult or take some control of the situation. It is the leader's job to write, as a way of distinguishing the "adult jobs" from the "kid jobs" and to help the children feel taken care of.

D. Feeling Words

Another large sheet of paper is taped to the wall and titled FEELING WORDS. The children are asked to come up with suggestions for this list. Staff can say, "We're making a list of feelings people have. What are some feelings you can think of?" One of the leaders writes the children's suggestions on the paper. Again, Bunny and Koko may help the children come up with feeling words.

Clinical note: Emphasis is on helping the children to identify as wide a range of feelings as possible and creating an encouraging and accepting atmosphere. It is also important to introduce the notion of mixed and complex feelings, to the extent that the children can developmentally understand.

This activity provides the opportunity to help the children distinguish behaviors (i.e., crying) from feelings (i.e., sad). There may be a discussion in the group about the differences between what your body feels, such as hunger, and an emotion, such as happiness.

Note: Both lists, of group rules and feeling words, are posted each week in the group room and may be added to from time to time.

E. Closure and Snack

After sitting in a circle again, the leaders should hand out snack and briefly summarize the two lists that the group members created today. It is important to leave approximately ten minutes at the closing of this and every group. Children are frequently reluctant to leave and, if possible, rushing them out should be avoided.

On this or any day, if the topic discussed in the group is particularly anxiety producing, the group members may ask for snack to be served early. Staff will have to think about and decide ahead how to deal with this, and probably the issue of what to do when a child hoards food to give to his or her family or those picking him or her up. When children come from high conflict and trauma, they often use food to self-soothe and/or take care of other people. Preferably, food is not taken away from group or shared with others—please see the rationale discussed in the section titled "Snacks and Snack Time" on pages 95-96.

After a leader asks each child to state something he or she liked and didn't like about group today, it is a good time to remind the children that the group meets again the following week at the same time in the same place. Artwork the children created should be placed in their folders before they leave the room.

LK Session 2

How I am Feeling: Same and Different

Goals

To introduce feelings, particularly associated with transitions and change

To continue to develop group cohesion

To introduce the topic of family and differentiation of self

Materials

Rules chart, posted in the group room

Feeling words chart, posted in the group room

Name tags and folders (kept in the leader's possession)

Plenty of paper, pencils, and markers

Bunny and Koko puppets

A soft object, such as a Nerf or Koosh ball

Skittles, stickers, or gummy bears (optional)

Procedure

A. Check-In

Once they are seated in a circle, each child gets a chance to "check in" and say a feeling word for how he or she is feeling right now, and asked to explain why he or she is feeling that way. The children can use the feeling words from the posted list created last week or a word of their own. Each child is also invited to tell about something he or she did over the weekend with family.

B. Rules Review

The group rules are reviewed by asking members to help Bunny and Koko understand the list prepared the previous week. Rules can be added if children suggest important ones that were missed. The leaders should once again explain the rules about confidentiality to reassure the children of safety in the group.

C. The Name Game

One group leader takes a soft object that can be thrown, such as a Nerf ball, says her or his name, and passes it to any other child, saying that child's name. The child then has to say her or his name and pass it to another child, saying that child's name. The leaders may have to encourage all the children to participate. This game should be fun and fast paced, like hot potato. All the children are asked to say their names once before the game is started. Bunny and Koko play the name game along with the leaders and children.

D. Group Activity: Family Drawing

Clinical note: The purpose of this activity is

- to help the child identify her or his family members and where she or he belongs in the group;
- to identify and assess the child's conflicts about or with each parent and other systems issues; and
- to help the child differentiate her or his individual family situation from that of other group members.

Each child is given a large piece of paper and provided with crayons and/or markers. The leader asks each group member to draw a picture of his or her family

Some children will have difficulty producing a simple drawing or drawing both parents' houses on one page. These difficulties should be noted and will be indicative of the degree of anxiety associated with the parental separation and family conflict.

The leaders monitor how each child is doing on the task. For example, if, after three to five minutes, a child has not begun a drawing, a leader might ask, "Who are you going to draw first?" or make another comment that will facilitate activity in the child. A leader may offer positive feedback to those children doing the activity: "Wow, I really like how you two are working so hard." This task can provoke some anxiety; leaders can offer the group supportive comments such as, "This can be a tough thing to do. Thank you all for trying your best." Reminding the group of the time remaining to draw is a useful prompt. Group members are given approximately fifteen minutes to complete this task. It is too distracting to have Koko and Bunny participate in this activity; they should be put off to the side before the beginning.

After the children have had time to complete the drawing (or enough time has been allotted to do so), each child is asked to talk to the group about her or his picture and family. Each child's reaction to the drawings should be noted. The following types of questions could be asked:

- Do you go back and forth between Mom's and Dad's houses?
- How is it for you to go back and forth?
- Would you like anything to be different in your family/house?
- What are some things you like about where you live?

E. How I Am Similar to My Family and How I Am Different

Clinical note: The purpose of this activity is to begin helping children to think about and tolerate issues of self-definition, which is central to the process of psychological individuation.

One leader begins this activity by saying:

> Now, let's do an activity so that we know a bit more about one another. I want each of you to think of some ways that you look like or act like someone else in your family. Maybe everyone in your family likes basketball or everyone in your family has brown hair.

This activity can be a bit difficult for some children. It is helpful to emphasize the physical characteristics and gender of the children's family members. To assist the group members, the leaders ask Bunny and Koko the same questions. The puppets should focus on and compare the physical attributes of family.

BUNNY: Everyone in my family has big ears, just like me!

KOKO: Everyone in my family has a loud voice like mine! We all talk like this!

The leader then asks the group to focus on ways they differ from family members:

> Now I want each of you to think of some ways that you are different from everyone else in your family. Maybe you are the only one in your family who plays soccer, or you are the only one who's shy, or everyone else in your family has brown hair but yours is yellow.

After each child has been given a turn to respond verbally to the questions of similarities and differences, the leaders encourage the children to do a drawing of what they have just described.

Clinical note: The leaders should take notice of which family member (if any) the child identifies with, and whether the child is able to identify anything separate of his or her own. It is likely that many children will not be able to do so. The leader's role is to suggest and validate the possibility of the child being just like other family members in some ways while being unique in other ways. The children should not be pressed further, beyond this suggestion. Their responses are diagnostic.

F. Closure and Snack

When the children are seated in a circle, the leaders hand out snack and briefly summarize similarities and differences between children in terms of their food preferences, in their living situations, and other issues that have arisen during group. It is important to leave approximately ten minutes for this at the closing of the group. Children are frequently reluctant to leave and, if possible, rushing them out should be avoided.

Clinical note: As with other activities, it is the leader who always serves the snacks and drinks. The children will of course offer to help, as a way of pleasing the adults and/or taking some control of the situation. Although these roles are comforting to the children, they are ones that should be carried out by the group leaders. Too often these children are caretakers of their parents and anxious to please others. In group they are encouraged to be children who are nurtured by adults. During snack, the process of reviewing similarities and differences is an important step toward identifying and validating a group norm that also supports differentiation.

As part of the closing ritual of the group, a leader asks each child to state something she or he liked and did not like about group today, reminds the children that the group will meet again the following week at the same time and location, and places any artwork in the children's folders before they leave.

LK Session 3

Feeling Words and Faces:
Who I Am

Goals

To introduce a language for feelings
To develop a communication tool, both about feelings and gradations of feelings
To develop a sense of self as separate

Materials

Note: All materials starred with an asterisk (*) are reproduced or described in the manual at the end of the session.

Rules chart, posted in group room
Feeling words chart, posted in the group room
Name tags and folders (kept in leader's possession)
Plenty of paper, pencils, markers, and crayons
Bunny and Koko puppets
Skittles, stickers, or gummy bears (optional)
*Sets of "Feeling Faces": five large, cut-out feeling faces—
happy, mad, sad, scared, and surprised

Procedure

A. Check-In

After sitting down in a circle, each child gets a chance to "check in" and say a feeling word for how she or he is feeling right now, and asked to explain why she or he is feeling that way. The children can use the feeling words from the posted list or use words of their own. Each child is also asked to tell about something she or he did on the weekend with family.

B. Identification of Feelings

There are five faces with expressions of feelings: happy, mad, sad, scared, and surprised. These have been cut out of the master sheet of paper and pasted on cardboard or other heavy paper and cut into separate pieces. One leader says, "Here are some feelings that kids have sometimes." The group members are asked to say what they think the feeling is represented on each face. This is fun to do as a guessing game that Koko and Bunny can participate in as well.

Note: Examples of these feeling faces are included in this book at the end of this session. It is suggested that the larger faces be introduced first. You may also choose to create your own.

C. Feeling Face Charades

After all the feelings have been identified, a game of charades of feelings is begun. The leader asks each child to show the rest of the group a feeling face while the other children watch and are encouraged to guess what feeling each child is displaying. Each group member is asked to charade at least one feeling face. Sometimes the children like to pair up to show a feeling. This is especially useful for the very shy child who is not comfortable initially participating on his or her own. Koko and Bunny can participate during the feeling face charade game but should be put aside before the next activity begins.

D. Favorite Animal Drawing

Clinical note: The children's emerging sense of individuation can be supported in this task, which involves identifying and discussing their favorite animals. The choice of animal also assists in diagnosis of the children's perception of their role in scripts.

Each child is asked to identify her or his favorite animal and draw it on a piece of paper. After the children have had some time to finish, each group member is asked to show her or his drawing and describe it. The leaders can ask the following types of questions:

- What is it about this animal that you really like?
- What can this animal do that you like?
- Is this an animal that only you like, or does someone else in your family really like this animal?
- What can this animal do that you can [or can't] do?

Koko and Bunny are not used in this particular activity because the children will often draw one of the puppets, saying that rabbits and monkeys are their favorite animals. Some children do this because they believe it will please the group leaders or puppets, and thus they will not think about their own wishes and feelings.

E. Closure and Snack

As part of the closing ritual of the group, snack is served to all of the children during the last ten minutes of group. One leader asks each child to share something he or she liked and did not like about group today. A token or reward, such as a Skittle, sticker, or gummy bear can be handed out to each child after he or she answers the questions. Leaders should remind the children that the group meets again the following week at the same time. Materials are placed in the children's folders before they leave.

HAPPY

MAD

SAD

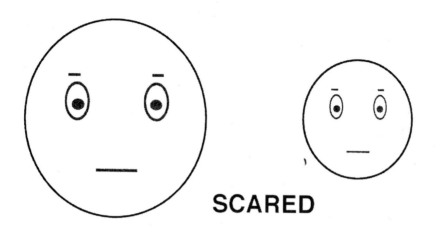

SCARED

SURPRISED

LK Session 4

Exploring Levels of Feeling

Goals

To further identify and express gradations of feelings
To develop a communication tool about feelings and gradations
of feelings

Materials

Note: All materials starred with an asterisk (*) are reproduced or described in the manual at the end of the session.

Rules chart, posted in group room
Feeling words chart, posted in the group room
Name tags and folders (kept in leader's possession)
Plenty of paper, pencils, markers, and crayons
Bunny and Koko puppets
*Sets of "feeling faces": five large, cut-out feeling faces—
happy, mad, sad, scared, and surprised
Skittles, stickers, or gummy bears (as optional positive reinforcers)

Procedure

A. Check-In

During "check-in," each child is asked to explain how she or he is feeling today. The children are invited to do this by either saying a feeling word or showing the group a feeling face, which the rest of the children have to guess. After the feeling is identified, the leader raises his or her hand and asks the child to explain why she or he is feeling that way. Koko and Bunny are asked to take a turn as well. Bunny,

Koko, and each child are also asked to share one thing they did this weekend with family.

B. Learning to Relax

Deep breathing is taught to the group by asking them all to put their hands on their tummies and breathe slowly in through their noses and out through their mouths. To make this a fun activity, the children are told to "smell the cookies" when they breathe in and to "blow out the candles" when they breathe out. It helps for the leaders to count out loud up to four as the children breathe in, reminding them to do it slowly, and to count out loud up to four as they breathe out, again reminding the children to blow slowly. This relaxation exercise is useful to do each week as part of the check-in routine, and at any time in the group when the children are agitated or having difficulty focusing. This is often the case at the end of the session.

The leaders can choose different children and have each child show the rest of the group how to do this relaxation exercise. Lots of positive reinforcement should be given to those trying to do this exercise; staff says "You are doing a great job with your breathing!" The children enjoy giving suggestions of other things to smell and blow, such as "smell the pizza and blow to cool it off." Bunny and Koko actively participate in this exercise. Koko does so in an exaggerated manner, while Bunny timidly tries it only because asked to by the group leader.

C. Gradations of Feelings

The leaders ask the members of the group to remind Koko and Bunny about the feeling words learned last week. A leader brings out the cut-outs of the five large feeling faces and asks the group what feeling words match the faces. Five small feeling faces, which match the large ones, are then introduced. The sets differ in size to show gradation of feelings, from "A REALLY BIG FEELING" to "a really small feeling." The leader describes the sets to the group, talking about how one is a really big happy feeling, and one is a really small happy feeling, continuing with all five feeling words. The group leader may illustrate by holding arms wide open to show a big feeling and hands close together to show a small feeling.

The leader asks the group if someone can show what a big happy feeling looks like and then asks the same child to also show a small happy feeling. Each child in the group is encouraged to show a big and small happy feeling. If the group seems able and willing to, then demonstrations of other big and small feelings can be done. Koko and Bunny should participate in this discussion, validating the children's feelings and efforts and giving examples themselves if the children are reluctant to do so. Remember, Koko will have difficulty expressing the small feelings, as Bunny will with showing big feelings.

D. Gradations of Feelings Activity

Clinical note: This activity helps children become aware that feelings can be experienced and acted upon in gradations. As a result, feelings are potentially less overwhelming and behavior is potentially more predictable and less frightening.

A group leader says: "Let's talk about when we have big feelings and small feelings. For example, what kind of a feeling do you have when you get a present you like?"

Leaders elicit feelings from the group by asking if someone would like to pick and show the feeling face that matches this example. It is expected that the feeling face would be a happy one. Validate the feeling shown, whether a big or small feeling face is chosen, and give an example of the opposite size to illustrate it. The same exercise is repeated by choosing another situation designed to elicit a different feeling. Koko and Bunny can participate in this discussion, chiming in when a situation is one that they have had.

To encourage the children to relate the big and small feelings to their own experiences, the leader shows the group one of the large feeling faces and asks, "Has anyone ever had a really big feeling like this one?" The leader may also ask the children if they have ever seen an adult with a "really big feeling."

The leader helps the children respond by reflecting each child's answer and reminding the group members to listen to one another. It may be helpful to have the drawing paper and materials available, as a way to help the children contain their anxieties and control their behaviors. These feelings can make the children uncomfortable, and some may act out their discomfort. The leader then gives the group an example, saying:

Okay, now, what if you got a present that you liked, sort of, or maybe it's nice but you already have one like it. Would your feeling be a big happy feeling or a small happy feeling?

After eliciting that smaller feeling, the leader encourages children to give examples of times they had small feelings, using the small feeling faces. It may be useful and helpful to the group if the leader takes the children's examples of big feelings and changes the situations to set the occasion for a small feeling to occur.

E. Charades of Feeling Gradations

The game of charades, incorporating the idea of big and small feelings, is initiated. The leader says to the children:

Let's play a game now so we can see really big feelings and really small feelings. I want each of you to think of a feeling of any size. It could be a really big happy, a really small sad, a really big mad, or a really small scared. Now, when it's your turn, you will show us this feeling, and it will be our job to guess which feeling it is and whether it's a big or small feeling.

As the children take turns in charades, Koko and Bunny help guess which feeling is being shown. The leader can prompt the children to elaborate on these feelings by asking:

What do you look like when this feeling gets bigger/smaller?
How can you tell when someone feels something a lot or just a little?
When people cry, how do they feel? Is it a big or small feeling?
How do people feel when they hit? Is it a big or small feeling?
What do people do when they're just a little mad? How about a really big mad?
Have you ever started out with a little feeling that got bigger? What happened?
Have you ever started out with a big feeling that got smaller? What happened?

F. Closure and Snack

During the last ten minutes of group, as the closing ritual of sitting in a circle and serving snack occurs, one leader asks each child something he or she liked and did not like about group today. A token or reward (Skittle, sticker, or gummy bear) may be handed out to each child after he or she answers each question. During snack, leaders should give a brief recap of today's discussion about big and small feelings and remind children that the group will meet again the following week at the same time. Materials should be placed in the children's folders before they leave.

HAPPY

MAD

SAD

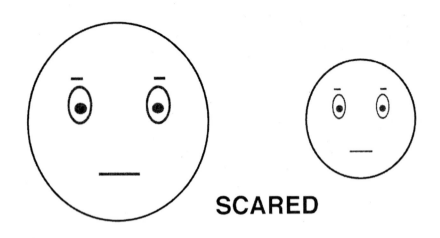

SCARED

SURPRISED

Managing My Good and Bad Feelings at One Time

Goals

To consolidate the idea of gradations of feelings
To help children articulate the experience of a good/bad split
To help children begin to work with possible integrations of a
good/bad‡ split

Materials

Note: all materials starred with an asterisk (*) are reproduced or described in the manual at the end of the session.

Rules chart, posted in the group room
Feeling words chart, posted in the group room
Bunny, Koko, and Max/Maxine puppets
Name tags and folders, kept by group leaders
Paper and drawing materials
*Measure of feelings chart, one for each child
Book: *Where the Wild Things Are,* by Maurice Sendak
Skittles, stickers, or gummy bears (optional)

---

‡Spontaneous feelings tend to be experienced by these children as reflecting their
"bad self" because they are not mirroring their parents' feelings and needs. Conversely,
when their own feelings are suppressed in order to support their parents, they experience
a "good self."

Procedure

A. Check-In

As they are seated in the circle, each child is asked to show a feeling face or say a feeling word to the others, illustrating how he or she is feeling. The children, Koko, and Bunny try to guess what the feeling word is and whether it is a BIG or small feeling. Each child is asked to explain why he or she is feeling that way. During his or her turn, everyone is still asked to share about something he or she did during the weekend with family.

B. Breathing Exercise

The deep-breathing exercise is reviewed to help them relax. The children, Koko, and Bunny are all asked to slowly "smell the cookies," to remind them to breathe in through the nose, then to "blow out the candles," to practice letting the breath out through the mouth. A leader can count out loud up to four to help them breathe slowly.

The leader can ask different children to show the rest of the group how to do this relaxation exercise, with lots of positive reinforcement given to all of those participating. The group reminds Koko and Bunny how to do the breathing and can have some fun thinking of other things to "smell" and "blow."

C. Measure of Feelings Activity

Clinical note: This activity helps children use the idea of levels of feelings to talk about their own experiences. Appreciating gradations of feelings can help children to develop beyond a polarized view in which feelings are either not felt or are out of control.

An enlarged photocopy of the Measure of Feelings Chart, which has five feeling faces, is handed out to each child with rulers and some feeling words (or feeling faces) written below. To explain this activity, the leader might say:

> What do you use when you want to measure something? Right!
> A ruler! Here are some rulers to help us measure our feelings
> [Pointing to the paper]. Use any color you want to show how

much of each feeling you have. This one is happy—see the feeling face underneath? Color up to here [Pointing to small] if you have only a little bit of happy feelings. Color up to here [Pointing at middle] if you have some happy feelings. Color up to here [Pointing at big] if you have lots of happy feelings.

The same description is given for each of the feelings shown on the paper. After the children have had a chance to work on it, each child is asked to show her or his drawing and explain about each feeling she or he colored. Koko and Bunny listen to everyone share, making positive comments about what the children say. The leader may facilitate a group discussion by asking if anyone else has had similar feelings to those being described. Koko and Bunny can add that they have feelings similar to what the children describe.

D. *Introduction of* Where the Wild Things Are

Clinical note: This activity helps children begin to be aware in a concrete way of the good/bad polarities that dominate and distort their understanding of self and others. When this issue is made concrete, the children can begin to work with the possibility of integration.

A leader asks the group if they recognize the book *Where the Wild Things Are.* Most of the children will. The leader continues:

Sometimes when children come to group they tell us that their feelings are very, very small, even invisible. Some kids tell us that their feelings are so big, so huge, that they feel like a wild thing. I'm going to read you a story about a little boy who has a lot of fun with wild things and is not afraid, but when he's tired he comes right back home.

A group leader then reads the book with lots of expression. The children should be able to draw or color during the story. After the story, the leader says, "Now, you see that Max (or Maxine so as not to be gender specific) had so many big feelings, didn't he/she? What were some of these wild feelings?" The leader helps the group to identify some of the big feelings that Max/Maxine had when he/she was with the wild things. These could include excitement, joy, strength, sadness, home sickness, and so on. The leader should end by noting that

Max/Maxine went off to the wild things because he/she was angry, so that must have been a big feeling as well.

A group leader continues, saying: "Now, you know, we have someone here who is kind of like Max/Maxine. He/she has lots of BIG feelings. In fact, he/she sometimes feels like a wild thing himself/herself. Do you know who that is? Koko!" Koko appears, behaving very actively. The children are given some time to respond. Then the leader says: "We also have someone in group who tells us she never feels like a wild thing. In fact, her feelings are very tiny and sometimes invisible! Do you know who that is? Bunny!" Bunny returns, behaving very timidly. The children are again given some time to respond. A leader asks the children, "Does anyone here ever feel the way Bunny does?" then asks "Does anyone here ever feel the way Koko does?" and responding to the group members by supportively acknowledging what they volunteer. The leader concludes by saying,

> You know, we've talked about having a lot of big feelings, like a wild thing, and we've talked about having small, invisible feelings. However, it seems like maybe people have big feelings sometimes and little feelings sometimes, and it's important to have both. We'll be able to talk more about that next week.

E. Closure and Snack

As is done each week, snack is served to all of the children as they sit in a circle at the end of group. The children are each asked to say something they liked and did not like about group today. A token or reward can be handed out to each child after he or she answers the questions. A leader should give a brief recap of today's discussion, perhaps asking the children whether they had ever heard the story before and what ideas or feelings they had about it. Leaders remind children that they will see them again the following week at the same time. Materials should be placed in the children's folders before they leave.

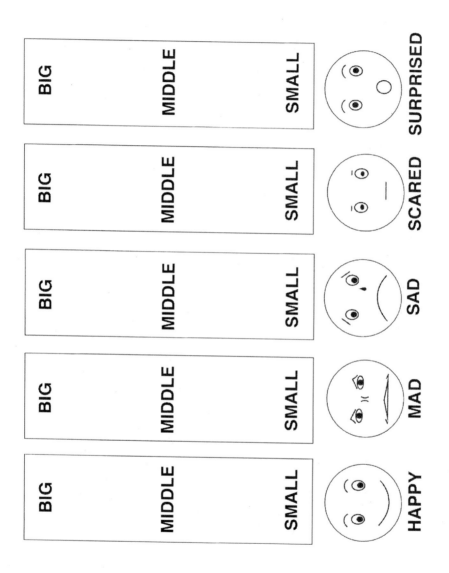

BIG	BIG	BIG	BIG	BIG
MIDDLE	MIDDLE	MIDDLE	MIDDLE	MIDDLE
SMALL	SMALL	SMALL	SMALL	SMALL
HAPPY	MAD	SAD	SCARED	SURPRISED

LK Session 6

Feeling and Being Me: Separate and Together

Goals

To consolidate a sense of constancy and cohesion in the group
To anchor children's ideas about a good/bad split in the feeling/
nonfeeling split that is identified in *Where the Wild Things
Are,* as personified by Bunny and Koko and integrated by
Max/Maxine

Materials

Rules chart, posted in the group room
Feeling words chart, posted in the group room
Another large piece of paper to tape to the wall
Plenty of paper, markers, and pencils
Bunny, Koko, and Max/Maxine puppets
Book: *Where the Wild Things Are*
Large flat bedsheet or blanket
Skittles, stickers, or gummy bears (optional)

Procedure

A. Check-In

The children are usually eager to show a feeling face and have the
others guess what the feeling word is. They are often talking about
this before sitting down to begin group. Once seated in a circle, each
child is given a turn and asked to show what the feeling looks like
when it is big and small and to explain why she or he is feeling that

way. Each child shares something she or he did over the weekend with family.

B. Breathing and Relaxation Exercises

The group members are asked to practice their deep breathing; the leaders ask the children for suggestions about what to "smell" and "blow." Koko and Bunny participate as well. Another relaxation exercise can be introduced to the group. For example, the leaders teach the children how to progressively tighten then loosen different muscles, such as those in fingers, toes, and shoulders.

C. Who's There?

Clinical note: The purpose of this activity is to help the children feel that they are part of the group in a pleasurable and appealing way.

The leader introduces today's activity as a game and says:

> To play the game, it will be very important to remember the faces and names of everyone who is here. Let's go around the group and each one will take a turn naming everyone. Put your name tags away.

After each child has done this, the leader explains that in this game, one child at a time is sent "over the mountain," which will mean out of the room with one of the leaders. Meanwhile, in the room with the rest of the group, one child is selected by the other leader to be "in the meadow," which means hiding under a blanket or sheet. With the help of the group, when the second child is safely curled up under the blanket or sheet, the first child and coleader are called back from "over the mountain" and the child must identify by name who is "in the meadow." When the child guesses, everyone lifts the cloth at the same time, so all of the children remain involved in the game. The children take turns until everyone has had a chance to play. Koko and Bunny can play along as well, though not the group leaders. It would be problematic if one adult hides under the cloth while the other was out of the room, and the children were thus unsupervised.

Any child has the right not to play. Reluctant children usually change their minds once the game is in progress. The other children should be encouraged not to tell the one who is "over the mountain" who is "in the meadow."

D. "Wild Things" Role-Play

Clinical note: This activity creates a working metaphor for the feeling/nonfeeling polarity, which these children need to integrate. Bunny embodies constricted nonfeeling. Koko embodies the feared out-of-control feeling. Both Bunny and Koko split off their feelings in different ways; neither has integrated or has gained flexible control of her or his feelings. Max/Maxine is the integrator. He/she can feel and control his/her feelings. He/she can go "where the wild things are" and then he/she can come home.

It is possible for this role-play to be videotaped, but only when everyone is "ready" to go on camera. This structured approach may heighten focus and seriousness in the role-players. The leader precedes the role-playing by staging a short puppet play that has Koko and Bunny trying together to remember very briefly the story of *Where the Wild Things Are* from the previous session. The following points should be highlighted:

> Max/Maxine goes to the land of the wild things when he/she gets angry.
> Max/Maxine enjoys being with the wild things.
> Max/Maxine can "stare into their yellow eyes" and say "No!" to the wild things.
> Max/Maxine can say good-bye to the wild things whenever he/she wants to and then go home.

The leader then introduces Koko's and Bunny's positions in relation to the land of the wild things. The leader might have Bunny say: "Oh, I'm afraid to go there. I would never go near those wild things! They're bad! If I went there, I could never go home again!" Koko might then say to Bunny: "You're silly! I go there all the time. I'm not scared! I don't even want to go home!"

The leader sets up a role-play using Max/Maxine, Bunny, and Koko; the book can be propped open for background scenery, if desired. The role-play is called "Bunny and Koko go where the wild things are and meet Max/Maxine." The following narrative is a guide for the leader's facilitation of the role-play:

> Koko decides to go where the wild things are. He wants Bunny for company. Bunny refuses. She's too scared. They work out a deal. Bunny says she'll stay in the boat and watch. When they arrive, Koko joins the wild things and their rowdiness gets out of control. Bunny hides in the boat and covers her eyes. Max/Maxine comes into the scene. Bunny opens her eyes. Max/Maxine joins Koko for a moment and then says that it's time to stop. He/she faces the wild things and "stares into their yellow eyes" and makes them stop. Koko stops because no one is left to prance around with. Bunny is very relieved. Max/Maxine says it's time to go home. He/she gets into the boat with Bunny. Koko is mad and stamps his foot. Finally, he, too, agrees to go home. They arrive safely home and are very happy.

This role-play should be set up with the leaders using the Max/Maxine, Bunny, and Koko puppets. The role-play is repeated without any puppets, using volunteers from the group to play each part, including that of the wild things. If there is time, the play can be repeated with the children taking turns playing different roles.

E. Closure and Snack

The group members may need another round of deep breathing as a way of calming down after this activity. Snack is not served until the children are in a circle and appear relatively calm. One leader asks each child what she or he liked and did not like about group today. A token or reward can be handed out to each child after she or he answers the questions. A leader gives a brief recap of today's discussion, including the ideas or feelings the children expressed in the role-plays and perhaps how exciting it was to pretend to be Bunny, Koko, and especially a wild thing! Leaders remind the children about meeting again the following week at the same time. Materials are placed in the children's folders before they leave.

LK Session 7

It's Okay to Be Different

Goals

To provide language for the polarity of feeling (bad-self) and nonfeeling (good-self)

To differentiate self from others' feelings and ideas

To continue exploring possible integration of feeling (bad-self) and nonfeeling (good-self)

Materials

Rules chart, posted in the group room

Feeling words chart, posted in the group room

Name tags and folders (kept in leader's possession)

Plenty of paper, markers, pencils, and crayons

Bunny, Koko, and Max/Maxine puppets

Book: *Where the Wild Things Are*

Other animal puppets for the children to use

Skittles, stickers, or gummy bears (optional)

Procedure

A. Check-In

The children will eagerly show a feeling face and want the others to guess what the feeling word is. Once seated, each child is given a turn and asked to show what the feeling looks like when it is big or small and to explain why he or she is feeling that way. Each child shares something he or she did over the weekend with family.

B. Relaxation Exercise

The group members are asked to practice their deep breathing; the leaders ask the children for suggestions about what to "smell" and "blow." The relaxation exercise in which the children tighten and loosen different muscles can be used in addition to, or instead of, the deep breathing. Koko and Bunny participate in all of these activities.

C. Introduction to Differentiation

Clinical note: This activity supports the children's awareness and tolerance of their qualities as individuals, separate from others in their families, especially when conflict threatens.

A leader introduces the next activity by saying:

> Remember, the other week we talked a lot about big feelings and small feelings. You may start to notice that your feelings are your very own and sometimes they're different than your mom's or dad's or your brother's or sister's. Let's talk about how you might be different in other ways. For example, no one looks exactly like her or his mom or dad.

At this point, Koko and Bunny can chime in and begin to model this activity. For example, Koko might say, "I have hair that's like my mom's color and eyes that mix up both Mom's and Dad's color." Bunny might say, "I have ears like my dad's and eyes like my mom's, but my whiskers look just like my very own and not like anyone else's." The leader prompts each group member for this kind of self/other identification and differentiation. Lots of positive feedback should be given to those who participate.

D. Bunny and Koko Have a Fight

Clinical note: This helps the children shift from thinking in terms of a good/bad split to thinking about a feeling/nonfeeling split and considering possible integrations.

To begin the story, a group leader says to the children: "You know, Bunny and Koko had a big fight yesterday. They asked if you guys could help them figure out which one of them is right. Are you willing to help them out?"

The leaders should not proceed until the children's attention is focused. The leaders then stage a puppet play using Koko and Bunny, in which the conversation is something like this:

KOKO: [Angrily] Bunny, you're a scaredy cat. Everyone thinks you're a goody-two-shoes! You're really a chicken!

BUNNY: [Whines] Koko, you're bad. Everyone knows you're bad—you're wild, and have wild friends, and you do wild things!

KOKO: I like doing wild things with my wild friends—at least I'm not invisible like Bunny! You're the one who is always hiding in the boat.

BUNNY: I'm smart because I'm not the one who always gets into trouble.

At this point, both puppets stop and turn to the children and ask for their opinions: "Who's right? What do you think?"

The leaders begin by reflecting and clarifying the children's ideas. This is followed by gentle challenges to their beliefs, such as maybe Bunny does feel invisible. Maybe Koko gets lonely when he gets lost with the wild things. The thrust of the challenge is to get the children to consider that neither Bunny's always being "good" nor Koko's always being "bad" is comfortable or realistic.

To enhance the success of this activity, it is helpful to write down the ideas the children come up with on a piece of paper taped to the wall. The children like to make lists, and it validates their ideas to have them written down. It is important for the leaders *not* to negate any ideas the children suggest.

After a short discussion, one leader brings both Bunny and Koko back to continue their argument, because, as they say disgustedly to the leader, "You can't decide, either!" After a brief exchange between Bunny and Koko, the other leader brings in Max/Maxine. The conversation may go as follows:

MAX/MAXINE: Hey, what are you guys fighting about?

BUNNY: [Tells her side of the story]

KOKO: [Tells his side of the situation]

MAX/MAXINE: [Laughs] You know what, you're both right and you're both wrong!

BUNNY: I'm confused. I don't understand.

KOKO: [Surprised] Hey, I don't understand. How can that be?

MAX/MAXINE: Well, it's not bad to have a lot of wild feelings, and it's not so good to keep them all inside! You have to do some of both, like me.

BUNNY: I still don't understand what you mean!

KOKO: Come on! Explain it to us again!

MAX/MAXINE: When I need to get wild, I have a lot of fun, like Koko, but when I'm getting too wild, I calm wild friends down and then I want to be more like Bunny. I guess I'm like Koko sometimes and like Bunny sometimes. I'm a Bunnmonkey!

E. The Children's Turn for Puppet Plays

When the leaders have completed the puppet play, the children are invited to conduct their own puppet plays about Bunny and Koko fighting. The children use different animal puppets of their choosing, provided by staff. It is recommended that one set of children at a time does this, with the rest of the group watching. The children can take turns using the other animal puppets and having a "fight" like Koko and Bunny did. The children may or may not choose to use Max/Maxine. The audience is invited to participate by describing the feelings in the plays as big or small, or they can get involved in the argument themselves by challenging statements that the puppets make. One of the leaders should use Max/Maxine as part of this audience participation process, having Max/Maxine provide compromises and suggestions as he/she did for Bunny and Koko.

F. Closure and Snack

At the end of group, the puppets are put away, the children are seated in a circle, and the leader serves snack. As is the ritual, a leader asks each child something she or he liked and did not like about group today, giving out a token or reward to each child after she or he answers the questions. A leader gives a brief recap of today's discussion, perhaps asking the children to consider how Koko and Bunny could settle their argument. Although the children's ideas are re-flected and supported, the leader may wish to suggest compromise resolutions as well as the "Say you're sorry" or "Stop fighting" sug-gestions that the children are likely to recommend.

The leaders remind the children that the group will meet again the following week at the same time, noting that they will do so four more times before group is over. Materials are placed in the children's fold-ers before they leave.

Going Back and Forth: Managing Transitions and Change

Goals

To heighten children's awareness and tolerance of feelings associated with transitions

To increase children's awareness of how they manage their feelings during transitions, particularly by polarizing feeling and nonfeeling

Materials

Rules chart, posted in the group room
Feeling words chart, posted in group room
Name tags and folders (kept in leader's possession)
Plenty of paper, markers, and pencils
Bunny, Koko, and Max/Maxine puppets
Books: *Where the Wild Things Are,* by Maurice Sendak and *Quick As a Cricket,* by Audrey Wood
Skittles, stickers, or gummy bears (optional)

Procedure

A. Check-In

The children will eagerly show a feeling face and want the others to guess the feeling word and whether it is a big feeling or a small feeling. Each child is given a turn and asked to show what the feeling would look like if it were big or small and to explain why he or she is feeling that way. Each child shares something he or she did over the weekend with family.

B. Relaxation

The group members are asked to practice their relaxation exercise, doing deep breathing or tight/loose muscles. Koko and Bunny participate in this as well.

C. Koko Puppet Play

Clinical note: The next two activities increase awareness and tolerance of feelings during the transition between parents or other difficult times.

The leaders conduct the following puppet play, asking children for feelings where indicated. Use one of the stories suggested, depending upon which is more appropriate and applicable for the situations experienced by most of the children in the group. The leader can create another one if neither story suits the needs of the majority of the group members.

> *Example 1:* Koko has to go from Mom's house to Dad's house. The story begins with Koko waking up at his mom's house on a school day and being told that this is his day to go to Dad. Koko complains that he feels tired and does not want to go to school.
>
> *Example 2:* Koko wants to see his dad. The story begins with Koko waking up at his mom's house on a school day and missing his dad. When he tells Mom, he is reminded that he cannot go to see his dad. Koko complains that he feels tired and does not want to go to school.

After telling the story, the leader asks the children what feelings Koko might have at that moment. They are encouraged to show the feelings on their faces. The leader reminds the group to consider whether the feelings are big or small.

Using either example, the story continues: At this point, Koko gets really angry. He goes "where the wild things are" and has a tantrum. He gets lost with the wild things. He tries to get them to stop, but he can't do it! He goes to school and gets in trouble there, too! His teacher calls him a "wild thing" and puts him in time-out.

> *Example 1:* When his dad picks him up, his teacher says that Koko has been wild. His dad gets mad at him, too.
>
> *Example 2:* When his mom picks him up, his teacher says that Koko has been wild. His mom gets mad at him, too.

Again, the children are asked to identify and show feeling faces, discussing whether they are big or small feelings. The story continues on:

> (With either example) Koko is embarrassed and still upset. He does not know why he feels so upset, but he does not want to do what his dad/mom wants. He tries to tell his dad/mom what to do, instead. Koko's dad/mom gets mad at him for acting up. Koko ends up "where the wild things are." He finds Max/Maxine, and Max/Maxine reminds him that Koko knows what to do. Max/Maxine supports Koko taming the wild things. Koko stares into their yellow eyes and says "NO!" to the wild things. Koko can then say good-bye to the wild things when he wants to and go home. Max/Maxine says he's/she's proud of Koko: "Good job, Koko!"

Clinical note: Make sure there is a reworking of the story and resolutions/closure. Leaders must provide containment at the end of the story and not leave Koko wild and crazy.

At the end of Koko's story, the children are again asked to identify the feelings and show the feeling faces, with clarification from leaders on whether these are big or small feelings. When the play is done, the leader summarizes all the feelings that Koko is holding and comments on how tired Koko must be and how hard it is to carry around so many feelings. Also, mention how much energy it takes to tame those wild things!

D. Bunny Puppet Play

The same puppet play is enacted, with Bunny as the central character. She may be making a transition from Mom's to Dad's house, or missing her mom because she does not see her.

Example 1: The story begins with Bunny waking up at her dad's house on a school day and being told that this is her day to go to her mom's. Bunny feels tired and wishes she could just stay in bed.

Example 2: The story begins with Bunny waking up at her dad's house on a school day and missing her mom. When she tells dad, she is reminded that she cannot go to see her mom. Bunny feels tired and wishes she could just stay in bed.

The children are asked to tell what feelings Bunny might have at that moment by using their words and showing feeling faces. The leader should comment that because Bunny does not show her feelings, sometimes it might be hard to know how she feels. The story continues:

(With either example) Bunny goes to school. Her tummy feels a little upset, but she tells herself it does not matter. She does her work anyway and is very well behaved.

At this point the story stops again, and the children are asked to use feeling words and feeling faces to identify Bunny's feelings. The leader helps them clarify whether they are big or small feelings. The leader may note that Bunny probably has a lot of feelings, but she would not go near the wild things. She stays in the boat with her eyes closed! She does not show her feelings. No one knows for sure how she feels. Again, the story continues:

(Using either example) When Mom/Dad comes to get Bunny from school, Bunny is very quiet. She has a stomachache from keeping all her feelings inside. It takes a lot of Bunny's energy to be able to keep everything held in, but it is hard work. She gets lonely sometimes, because no one knows what she really feels.

The leader then asks the children for ideas to help Bunny let out her feelings. Bunny should listen to the ideas and try them, if possible. Max/Maxine should come to encourage Bunny to try these ideas, assuring her it is a good thing to do. Max/Maxine may have to encourage the children to offer these ideas.

Clinical note: Make sure there is a reworking of the story and resolutions/closure. Leaders must provide soothing and support at the end of the story and not leave bunny shut down and somatic.

(With either example) Bunny tries the ideas the children suggest and says she feels much better having expressed some of her feelings. She is pleasantly surprised to find her stomachache has gone away, and she feels less lonely.

The leader should close the puppet play by reflecting and summarizing Bunny's and Koko's feelings. The point should be made that sometimes your feelings feel really big and wild, and sometimes they feel so tiny that they are almost invisible! The leader adds that next time the group will see if Max/Maxine can help Bunny and Koko with all their feelings.

Some other possible stories could include Bunny hearing someone in her family saying negative things about one of her parents. Koko may overhear an argument between family members or his parents. The children may come up with their own ideas for stories about situations they have encountered. If there is time, another story may be told in a similar way as the others.

E. Closure and Snack

Toward the end of group as the children sit down in a circle, snack is served. The children are asked to say what they liked and did not like about group today and given a token or reward for responding. A leader gives a brief recap of today's discussion and tells the children that the group will meet again the following week at the same time, reminding them about how many sessions are left.

As with other group sessions, if the group would benefit more from a calming activity or if the group is anxious and wants snack early, then a book or poem can be read during snack. Materials should be placed in the children's folders before they leave.

LK Session 9

Managing When Parents Fight

Goals

To help children identify feelings associated with their parents' fighting

To increase children's awareness of how they manage their feelings during parental fights

To help children achieve some cognitive mastery and distance from the fighting

Materials

Rules chart, posted in the group room

Feeling words chart, posted in the group room

Name tags and folders (kept in the leader's possession)

Plenty of paper, pencils, and markers

Bunny, Koko, and Max/Maxine puppets, and the book *Where the Wild Things Are*

Other animal puppets for the children to use

Skittles, stickers, or gummy bears (optional)

Procedure

A. Check-In

The children are comfortable and familiar with the group routine and will eagerly show a feeling face and want the others to guess what the feeling word is and whether it is a big feeling or a small feeling. Once the group is seated and ready, each child is given a turn and asked to show what the feeling would look like if it was big or small and to explain why she or he is feeling that way. Each child shares something she or he did on the weekend with family.

B. Relaxation

The group members are asked to practice their deep breathing; the leaders ask the children for suggestions about what to "smell" and "blow." Koko and Bunny participate in all of these activities.

C. Bunny, Koko, and Conflict

Clinical note: This activity helps children begin to talk about and tolerate gradations in the feelings that are aroused by conflict.

One leader begins by telling the children:

> You know, Bunny told me about something that happened yesterday that really bothered her. She was at school and she saw two kids fighting. I asked her what that was like for her. Guess what she said?

After the children respond and become engaged with the material, the leader with Bunny has the puppet say: "Well, you know me! At first, I said it was fine, that it didn't bother me at all. But it did bother me! I felt a little scared and a little worried." At this point, Koko jumps in and says loudly: "It bothered me! It made me mad! I wanted to stop it right away! My parents fight and I don't like it! Not at all!"

The leader follows with a brief discussion that allows the children to talk openly about fighting and how it makes them feel. The children are encouraged to identify gradations of feelings, both in themselves and in the people who are in conflict. For example, if a child says "My parents yell at each other," the leader will prompt him or her to say how he or she feels when this happens and whether this is a big or small feeling. If a child says, "That happened at my school. These two kids were fighting at recess," the leader should encourage him or her to say how it felt to see this and whether his or her feelings were big or small.

D. Puppet Play of a High-Conflict Situation

Clinical note: This activity helps the children identify their feelings about conflict and gain support and validation from one another and from the leader.

The leader introduces the role-play: "Has anyone ever been with grown-ups when they were having a fight about something?"

The leader attempts to elicit a brief idea for a role-play from one of the children's responses to this question. When a simple play has been formulated, the leader asks the child who volunteered the idea if he or she would like to act out the play using puppets (*not* Koko, Bunny, or Max/Maxine). If the child does not wish to do the play, leaders may ask for volunteers.

A leader facilitates the role-play, stopping at appropriate times to discuss whether small or big feelings are being illustrated. Particular attention should be paid to the children's feelings during the fighting. The leader should also focus the children's attention on what the puppet *believes* she or he has to do during the fighting. Prompts that a leader could use include the following:

> What could (puppet representing the child) do when the adults are fighting?
> What could (same puppet) say when the adults are fighting?
> Does this help (same puppet) to feel safe?
> What would happen if (same puppet) did something different? (the leader may have to suggest ideas)
> Is there any other way for (same puppet) to feel safe?
> What could (puppets representing grown-ups) do instead of fighting?

The leader's task is to supportively reflect what the puppet is feeling, doing, and trying to achieve. In this same context, the leader must help the children to identify what is and is not possible. For example, a leader may say:

> Sometimes Koko thinks he can stop the fighting, but Koko is a child and children can't make grown-ups stop fighting. How does Koko feel when he wants to make something happen and he can't do it?

Another possibility is:

> Sometimes Bunny wants to pretend that there is no fighting, but the fighting is really happening. What is it like for Bunny to wish so hard for something to disappear? Does she sort of disappear instead? How does Bunny feel then?

The leader needs to make time to either facilitate an alternative resolution puppet play about how the child would like things to get worked out or move on to a new puppet play with a different child. If an alternative resolution puppet play is chosen, it is important that children identify realistic considerations and feelings associated with the wished-for alternative.

Clinical note: It is very important that the puppet plays of conflictual situations are reworked so the children are not left with images of unresolved conflict. Also, when discussing situations that are so close to the children's real lives, it is important to not further tarnish the child's view of a parent or loved one.

E. Closure and Snack

Once the puppets are put away and the children are seated in a circle, snack is served to them. The children may ask for snack earlier because of the material covered this week. It is likely that this activity will generate a lot of feelings, especially anxiety. It can be useful at this time to do some deep breathing, or practice tightening and loosening muscles as a way to calm down. The leader can also read aloud some children's poetry that is funny and appealing to both boys and girls or a picture book that has an entertaining story.

The leader asks each child to state something he or she liked and did not like about group today, handing out tokens or rewards as the children respond if this is part of the closing ritual of the group. A leader should give a brief recap of today's discussion, perhaps remembering how the characters in the story settled their arguments.

Leaders should remind children that the group will meet again the following week at the same time, noting how many meetings are left before group is over. Materials are placed in the children's folders before they leave.

LK Session 10

Safety Planning and Ways of Coping

Goals

To help children think about their own safety
To develop plans for keeping safe

Materials

Rules chart, posted in group room
Feeling words chart, posted in group room
Plenty of paper, markers, and crayons
Name tags and folders, kept in leader's possession
Bunny, Koko, and Max/Maxine puppets, and the book, *Where the Wild Things Are*
Picture to color of adults fighting or another scene relevant to the children in group (use enlarged photocopies of pages 126 and 141)
Other animal puppets for the children to use
Skittles, stickers, or gummy bears (optional)

Procedure

A. Check-In

Comfortable and familiar with the group routine, the children will be ready to sit down and eagerly show a feeling face, wanting the others to guess what the feeling word is and whether it is a big feeling or a small feeling. Each child is given a turn and asked to show what the feeling would look like if it was big or small and explain why he or she is feeling that way. Each child shares something he or she did over the weekend with family.

B. Relaxation

The group members are asked to practice their deep breathing; the leaders ask the children for suggestions about what to "smell" and "blow." The leader can also suggest practicing relaxing by doing the tight/loose muscles exercises. Koko and Bunny participate in all of these activities.

C. Picture of Conflict

The leader passes out a picture of a scene that represents a situation the group members are familiar with. This may be one of the examples given in this book, such as the picture of the child being pulled by two adults or the one with a child in the middle of adults arguing (see pages 126 and 141). The leader may also create one that is more relevant to the situations the children in the group have experienced, such as incarceration of a parent or substance use. The same picture is given to all the group members for them to color.

As the children are coloring, the leader can initiate a discussion about the contents of the picture and the "story" that accompanies it. Questions can be asked of the group, such as:

> What do you think is happening in the picture?
> Why is this going on?
> How does the child feel? Is this a big or small feeling?
> How does the adult feel? Is this a big or small feeling?
> What could the adults do differently?
> Is there anything the child could do?

Depending on the ages and developmental levels of the children in the group, it may be fun to have the children add story balloons or write on the picture what they think the people in the picture would be saying. Koko and Bunny join the discussion but will not lead the conversation in any particular direction.

Toward the end of the activity, it is important to turn the conversation around to what *should* be happening, or alternative endings to the story that are safer and more appropriate. Although some children may come up with possibilities, it may be the leader who has to suggest ways the story invoked by the picture could involve less conflict or be resolved.

D. Puppet Play of Picture

If there is time, or if the leader finds it useful, the children can be invited to use puppets (not Bunny or Koko) to act out the scene they colored in the previous exercise. After creating the scene involving the conflict, it is imperative that the scene is reworked and an alternative ending is found and enacted with the puppets.

E. Safety Plans

Using a large sheet of paper taped to the wall, the leader introduces the activity by telling the children:

> We've talked a lot about different times that kids don't feel safe, for instance, if adults are arguing or people are scaring you. Now let's make a list of ways that kids can keep themselves safe. Who has some ideas?

As the leader writes down the suggestions the children make, she or he can elaborate and ask other questions to clarify the choices children have in these unsafe situations. Koko and Bunny can help, especially to be sure that important safety items are included. Ideas should include the following:

- Finding a safe adult to go to—this includes situations in and out of the home, such as at school or in a shopping mall.
- Calling 911—when and why the children should consider doing this.
- Identifying safe people inside and outside the home—this will include neighbors, teachers, and police.
- Finding safe places to go, such as a neighbor's home, the office at school, or in a room with the door locked, if necessary.

The children will need to be reassured by the leader that these measures are for their own safety and that it is not a child's job to stop adults from drinking, fighting, or engaging in other unsafe or inappropriate activities. Koko and Bunny can assist with this discussion; for example:

BUNNY: I don't know if I could yell for help. What if I got in trouble for yelling?

LEADER: It will be scary to yell, Bunny, but it's a good way to keep yourself safe.

KOKO: I'm good at yelling! I can do that!

LEADER: You do that well, Koko, but remember you're going to yell to get help from a grown-up.

KOKO: I won't have to call the police! I can make them stop! I'm strong!

LEADER: You are strong, Koko, but stopping a fight is a job for the police.

BUNNY: I'm not supposed to use the phone. My dad will get mad if I do that.

LEADER: Well, he might, but you have to call the police if adults are throwing things or hurting each other. The police will keep things safe.

This discussion can evoke quite a bit of anxiety for the children, so it is useful to have coloring paper and materials available to help them contain some of the big feelings that this discussion may evoke.

F. Closure and Snack

While the children are seated in a circle, snack is served to them. The children may ask for snack earlier because of the material discussed in the safety plan, so the leader may decide to serve snack as the list is being generated and discussed.

After the list is completed or the children finish snack, it can be helpful do some deep breathing or practice tightening and loosening muscles. The leader can also read aloud some children's poetry that is funny and appealing to both boys and girls or a picture book that has an entertaining story.

The leader asks each child to state something he or she liked and did not like about group today, handing out tokens or rewards as the children respond if this is part of the closing ritual of the group. The group is reminded that they will meet again the following week, same time and place, noting how many sessions remain before group is over. Materials are placed in the children's folders before they leave.

LK Session 11

Masking Feelings:
My Inside and Outside Self

Goals

To help the children begin to anticipate termination of group

To heighten children's consciousness of having to hide feelings when parents are involved in conflict

To provide support for the feelings of shame about self that result when children cannot be completely open and honest with each parent

Materials

Note: All materials starred with an asterisk (*) are reproduced or described in the manual at the end of the session.

Rules chart, posted in the group room
Feeling words chart, posted in group room
Plenty of paper, markers, and crayons
Name tags and folders, kept in leader's possession
Bunny, Koko, and Max/Maxine puppets and the book, *Where the Wild Things Are*
*Group of children sheets
Other animal puppets for the children to use
Skittles, stickers, or gummy bears (optional)

Procedure

A. Check-In

The children are comfortable and familiar with the group routine and will eagerly show a feeling face, wanting the others to guess what the feeling word is and whether it is a big feeling or a small feeling. Each child is given a turn and asked to show what the feeling would look like if it were big or small and to explain why she or he is feeling that way. Each child shares something she or he did over the weekend with family.

B. Relaxation

The group members are asked to practice their relaxation exercises, with the children suggesting what to smell and blow or doing deep breathing or tight/loose muscles. Koko and Bunny participate in this as well.

C. Getting Ready to Say Good-Bye

Clinical note: This activity helps the children begin to anticipate termination (the next session) and to be able to say good-bye in a way that reflects appreciation of the relationship and the potential for constancy (i.e., that others will be held in memory).

After check-in, the leader reminds the group:

> We have been meeting together for quite a while now. Next time we get together will be our last time. So, let's start by making something that will help us remember each other and our time together in group.

The leaders pass out the "group of children" sheets and invite the children to color each figure in. The group leader will need to produce sufficient enlarged photocopies of the child figure so that each can be named for a child in the group. Each child will be provided with one sheet that contains figures that represent all group members. The group leader can ask the children to choose a figure to represent each person in the group and tell them what name to write. The enlarged photocopies should include a figure for each leader, Koko, Bunny, and Max/Maxine. Include figures for children who are missing or dropped out of the group. The time spent on this activity should be limited; the intention is to begin the activity this session and finish it during the final session. When the time is up, the sheets should be collected and placed in each child's folder. The children are reassured that they will be able to finish their coloring next week and take this and their other pieces of artwork home on the last day of group.

D. Bunny Learns More About Expressing Feelings

Clinical note: This activity increases the children's awareness of their strategies for masking feelings and to provide support for the associated shame about not feeling able to be openly real or honest.

The leaders begin talking to the children about how sometimes what people feel inside does not match the feelings they show on the outside. The leader can give an example by saying: "Remember a time when you got a present you didn't like? What were you feeling? Maybe someone gave you a toy for little kids. Did you think 'yuck! I don't want this?'"

The children can be asked to show a feeling face for when they get a present that they do not like. The leader goes on: "But you can't really tell the person who gave you the present that you don't like it, can you? You have to say thank you anyway. Do you know why?"

The children are asked to give ideas about why they do not tell how they really feel. They are able to provide answers, saying it would be rude or hurt someone's feelings. Continuing the discussion, a leader says:

> Right! It wouldn't be nice to tell someone you didn't like his or her present. It would hurt his or her feelings. Usually you have to just say "thank you" and look on the outside as if you like the present, even though you really don't.

Bunny joins the discussion. The leader tells the children: "This is just like what happened to Bunny the other day! Do you want to hear about it?" The leader should not proceed until the group has focused their attention on Bunny, who then proceeds to tell her story hesitantly and with appropriate feelings.

Well, see, what happened was, my mom said a bunch of really mean things about my dad. When I heard this I felt sad and upset inside! But I didn't show my feelings to my mom. I kept them inside. On the outside, I pretended I didn't care. My mom didn't know how I felt.

At this point, it is the leader's task to encourage the children to help Bunny understand what happened to her. The group can be asked to guess and show feeling faces for Bunny's inside and outside feelings. The leader could then look confused and ask the group: "Well, how come Bunny didn't show her inside feelings?" or "What would happen if Bunny was sad on the outside?" It is important to then clarify with the group when and where Bunny could express these feelings. The leader can ask the children: "So where could Bunny let out her inside feelings, so she doesn't get a tummy ache?"

It is important to communicate to the group the following:

Bunny wasn't bad. It is sometimes important to not show on the outside the feelings you have on the inside as a way to stay safe.

Bunny's mom might have gotten mad or upset if Bunny had shown her inside feelings.

Does Bunny ever get lonely, hiding her inside feelings? Is there anyone she can be with and not hide her inside feelings (i.e., a pet, sibling, or with a parent at one time but not another time)?

What might Bunny have liked to do? Can she ever say, "Please don't say mean things about my dad?" Is that too scary? Can Bunny whisper it to herself or to a safe friend?

Maybe Mom needs help in understanding that when she says mean things about Dad, it makes Bunny feel sad. Should a grown-up talk to Mom?

Clinical note: Leaders should be alert to children's wishes to enlist the leaders' assistance in talking to parents.

E. Koko Learns More About Expressing Feelings

Following the preceding activity Koko joins in by saying:

Well, wait 'til you hear what happened to me. My dad was doing his work and said not to bother him. I felt sad inside, because I wanted to play with him. So I went and made lots of noise and looked happy on my outside! Boy, did I get in trouble! My dad didn't know I felt mad and lonely on the inside, that I just wanted his attention. I didn't tell him how I really felt.

At this point, it is the leader's task to help the children help Koko understand what happened to him. The group can be asked to guess and show feeling faces for Koko's inside and outside feelings. The leader could then look confused and ask the group: "Well, how come Koko didn't show his inside feelings?" or "What would happen if Koko was mad on the outside?" Then it is important to clarify with the group when and where Koko could express these feelings. The leader can ask the children: "So where could Koko let out his inside feelings, so he doesn't get in trouble?" It is important to communicate the following to the group:

Koko really wants his dad to pay attention to him, and that's okay. It isn't bad for Koko to want his dad's attention.

Maybe there are other ways to get attention. What ideas do the children have?

Maybe a grown-up needs to help Dad understand that Koko feels mad and lonely when Dad doesn't pay attention to him.

Clinical note: Again, the leaders need to make it clear that they can talk to the children's parents.

The children are asked to think about times they, too, did not show their inside feelings on the outside. To begin this discussion, the leader can give prompts such as:

Does anyone ever feel like they have to pretend or hide the way they are really feeling?

Does anyone in the group ever feel like Bunny or Koko did?

Does anyone in the group ever hide their inside feelings like Bunny and Koko did?

If there is time, the leader may invite children to create a puppet or role-play using these ideas. There should be some discussion of what

Bunny and Koko should do the next time they are not sure if they should show their inside feelings.

F. Closure and Snack

As is the ritual, snack is served to all of the children at the end of the group session, when they are sitting down in a circle. Again this week, the children may ask for it earlier because of the material covered. It can be useful for the children, as a group, to do some deep breathing. During snack, the leaders might close with the leader reading a poem or book aloud.

One leader asks each child something she or he liked and did not like about group today, handing out a token or reward to each child after she or he answers the questions. A leader should give a brief recap of today's discussion, perhaps remembering situations where inside feelings could be shown on the outside.

Leaders should remind children that the group will meet again the following week at the same time, noting that next week is the last time the group will meet together. Materials should be placed in the children's folders before they leave.

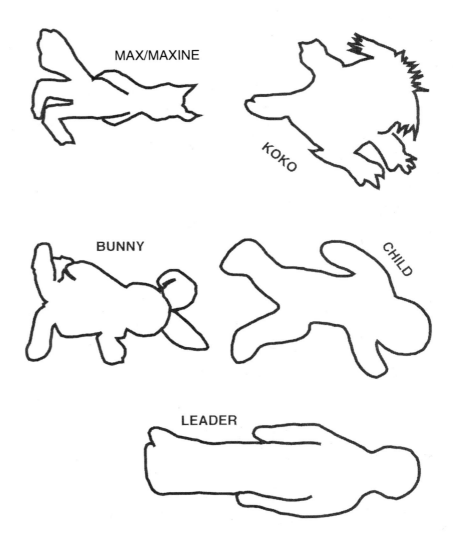

MAX/MAXINE

KOKO

BUNNY

CHILD

LEADER

LK Session 12

Remembering and Saying Good-Bye

Goals

To provide a positive termination experience

To help children consolidate their ideas and feelings about their parents' separation and/or conflict

To help children consolidate their feelings of support gained from being in a group with others in similar situations

Materials

Rules chart, posted in the group room

Feeling words chart, posted in the group room

Name tags and folders (kept in leader's possession)

Plenty of paper, markers, and pencils

Bunny, Koko, and Max/Maxine puppets and the book, *Where the Wild Things Are*

"Group of children" sheets from the previous week

Poster board for group

Leader's previously prepared ideas for "One thing I will remember about you, and one thing I wish for you" activity (see notes for this activity at end of session)

Party food

Procedure

A. Check-In

The children are comfortable and familiar with the group routine, and will eagerly show a feeling face, wanting the others to guess what the feeling word is and whether it is a big feeling or a small feeling.

Each child is given a turn and asked to show what the feeling would look like if it was big or small and to explain why he or she is feeling that way. This week, the children are also asked to show a feeling face about today being the last group. Each child still shares something he or she did over the weekend with family.

B. Relaxation Exercises

The group members practice their deep breathing, using the children's suggestions about what to "smell" and "blow." Koko and Bunny participate in this and may also ask the children about other situations where the breathing or tight/loose muscle activity might be helpful to use, outside of the group.

C. "Group of Children" Activity

After check-in is finished, the leaders pass out the "group of children" sheets from the previous session. Children should be given time to complete their sheets, coloring in the rest of the figures as they wish. While the children are working, the leaders, with Koko and Bunny, can note the children who have attended the group consistently and remember those that were not able to stay enrolled in the program. "It's been nice having John and Jane in group each week. It's too bad that Sally couldn't continue coming to group. It was nice having her here. Everyone brings something special to group."

If there is time, the children can be asked to list three feeling words that they like. These can be copied off of the group's posted feeling words chart. A feeling face can be added too, or drawn instead of the feeling word. Some children may want to copy some of the group rules off of the list created in the earlier session.

D. A Letter to Grown-Ups

Clinical note: This activity helps children gain a sense of having learned or understood something that belongs to each of them individually and to the group collectively.

The material that children contribute here is also diagnostically useful, clarifying for the leaders what might need to be discussed with each child's parents during collateral work. A leader can begin the activity by saying:

> We have talked about a lot of things in this group. Let's pretend that we are going to write a letter to your grown-ups. We aren't really going to send it, or show it to them, or anything like that. We could just write it and then throw it away! But let's pretend we were going to tell them what (divorce, fighting, drinking, people leaving for a long time) are like for kids! Just some stuff that parents ought to know. Remember, this letter isn't for sending. It will be private.

The leader can elicit statements from children by prompting with memories of things that children disclosed during previous sessions. Bunny and Koko can participate in the discussion, helping the group by remembering what was said in other sessions. The leader will write this up on the poster board or piece of paper posted on the wall, beginning like this:

> Dear grown-ups (or parents),
>
> Here's some stuff we think you should know! (continuing from there with the children's contributions)

It is also possible to do this activity at an earlier session, right before a parent group meeting is held, in which case explain to the children that the parents will see the letter. The leader tells the children:

> Your parents are coming in this week, and they'll be in a group just like you. They won't get snacks like we do, but they'll meet Koko and Bunny. Let's write them a letter to tell them what kids think about families and fighting and divorce. Here, I'll be your secretary and do all the writing.

Taking the pen and poster board or large paper, the group leader starts the letter:

> Dear parents,
>
> Here are some things that kids want you to know...(continuing with the contributions from the children)

The children are reassured that no names will be on the letter and the parents will not be told who said what. The leader promises the group members "You can tell your parents what you said if you want to, but we won't tell them." This letter becomes a very powerful tool in working with the parents. The children often ask their parents if they saw the letter and tell them what they contributed to it anyway.

E. Remembering and Saying Good-Bye

Clinical note: This activity provides children with the experience of being "held in mind" and to understand that they will continue to be "held in mind" after termination.

The leader says to the group: "Since we won't be meeting together after today, I'd like to give each of you two things: a memory and a wish." Each leader then focuses on one child at a time, sharing "one thing I will remember about you" and "one thing I wish for you" (see notes at the end of this session). Koko and Bunny are included, with the leaders mentioning what they will remember about, and wish for, each puppet.

The children are encouraged to add what they will remember about both Koko and Bunny, as well as any wishes they have for them. Max/Maxine can be helpful here, to remind the group members how Koko and Bunny used to be when they first came to group and how much they have changed. Koko and Bunny chime in with the leaders as they tell each child the memory and wish they have for her or him.

F. Snack, Closure, and Good-Bye

After the children are in a circle and have been served snack the leaders pass out all of the material in their folders. The folders will be taken home at the end of this session. The leaders ask the children to each share one thing they will remember about group. Or, the children can be asked to say one thing they liked about being in this group (not just today) and anything they did not like about being in this group (something they wished had been different about it).

If there still is time, the group can play "Over the Mountain/In the Meadow." Games are helpful because they provide some structure at a time when children are likely to regress. If the level of agitation is too high, the leaders may choose to read a few final and calming poems or stories. Before it is time to go, the leaders should make sure each child has his or her folder and has been told good-bye. Some children may decline to take their folders home because it will be seen by a parent who might get upset about its contents, in which case they can leave it with the group leader if they choose.

Clinical notes for "one thing I will remember about you, one thing I wish for you": It is important for the leaders to identify something special about each child. This trait should be recognizable and believable for the child, and one that she or he can feel good about. Because this sometimes requires careful thought, it is very useful to make sure the remarks are prepared ahead of time. For example, for a child who has been disruptive and distractible, or for a nonparticipating, silent child, it might be appropriate to say, "I will remember how brave you were for coming to group, when it was so hard to talk about feelings." No two children should be given the same comment. The wishes should also be identified ahead of time and should not exacerbate a child's sense of helplessness. For example, it is not helpful to wish for an end to the parents' conflict. Wishes should include ideas that are possible for the child to master. For example, "I wish that you might find a person or place that will help you feel safe showing your inside feelings," or "I wish that when you decide to be a mom(dad) you will be able to give your little girl or boy lots of attention."

LK Session Tips and Guidelines

PUPPET ETIQUETTE AND PUPPET BIOGRAPHIES

There are a few important reminders for using the puppets in the program. The puppets are introduced and treated as group members. The group leaders should switch off being Koko and Bunny each week, so neither adult becomes associated with either puppet or its personality. This holds true for Max/Maxine as well. The leaders are the only ones who can use the puppets. It takes away from their mystique if the children are allowed to use them. Also, constant arguments would occur about who got to use which puppet, taking time and energy away from the curriculum. Opportunities are provided during activities in the program for the children to use other puppets.

The puppets each have their own personality traits. It is not necessary for the group leaders to use anything except their regular voices when portraying Koko, Bunny, and Max/Maxine. It is very difficult to use a different voice for the entire group session and to remember from week to week what each one sounded like. The children will be confused if Koko has a deep voice one week and a high squeaky voice the next.

Similarly, the focus should be on how Koko and Bunny interact with the world, not what the problems are in either of their families. The children identify with the puppets because of how they describe themselves and each other. The more specific the information given about either puppet's family, the more complicated it will be for the group leaders to remember what they have said about Koko and Bunny from session to session. However, if most of the children live with a relative, not a birth parent, then an aunt or grandparent might also raise Koko or Bunny. If most of the group members have or still live with an adult who abuses substances, then the leaders may decide to have that be true for one of the puppets as well. Details beyond this become cumbersome. The stories about the puppets given in the curriculum should be changed to meet the needs of the majority of the children.

Koko and Bunny become important members of the group. They can be used to elicit participation, by asking the children to teach Bunny and Koko about certain concepts. If the puppets participate, the children are more likely to as well. Remember to make the focus of Koko and Bunny their emotions and experiences, not facts about their lives. Koko's and Bunny's behaviors and feelings should initially be exaggerated, so that as the group goes on and they learn the material, the changes in Koko and Bunny will be noticeable.

The three primary puppets used in this model have their own personalities and purposes that are outlined here. Max/Maxine is a young boy or girl, and the puppet used is designed to look like the character in the book *Where the Wild Things Are.* Koko is a monkey, though it could be a gorilla or ape puppet. Bunny is a rabbit; the puppet can be any color or style but should be this animal. Each of them has a particular way of being and behaving, which is described in the biographies that follow.

Max/Maxine

Max/Maxine is the integrator. With his/her charm and mischievous ways, he/she joins the group after a few weeks to help Koko, Bunny, and the children begin to synthesize their range of feelings. The children recognize him/her as the character in the book *Where the Wild Things Are,* and are delighted to see him/her come alive in the form of a puppet. To avoid gender stereotypes, it is useful for this puppet to be assigned as either a girl or a boy as the group composition warrants. Though he/she plays an important role, the children do not view him/her as their peer, unlike Koko and Bunny. Max/Maxine is not one of the group leaders, either. He/she is always seen as a child and in his/her playful way his/her function is to teach all of the group members, but primarily Koko and Bunny, what to do with their feelings.

Max/Maxine understands that Koko has big feelings that sometimes get out of hand and that Bunny has difficulty expressing her feelings. Max/Maxine comes to help when Koko finds himself trapped in the land of the wild things. He/she helps Koko learn how to control the wild things and along with the group leaders teaches Koko and the children safe and appropriate ways to express big feelings. Max/Maxine is there to encourage Bunny to do things that may be scary or involve risk taking. With Max's/Maxine's assistance, Bunny begins to take chances and express a wider variety of feelings.

As the integrator, Max/Maxine helps Koko, Bunny, and the children combine the qualities exhibited by both puppets. He/she does this by explaining to the group that feelings are not right or wrong, but there are appropriate and inappropriate ways to express them. His/her appearance in the group process coincides with times that Koko and Bunny are stuck in their own ways and need to learn new skills to move forward. If used to his/her potential, Max/Maxine could be included in the discussion at other times, if the children asked for his/her input or could benefit from his/her facilitation of a discussion.

Koko

Although the book refers to Koko as "he" or "him," Koko is not necessarily male. It would be unfortunate for him to be thought of or labeled as a boy. He is a charismatic member of the group, and boys and girls alike can relate to his experiences and expressions.

Koko is an energetic and very mischievous monkey who likes to play and have lots of fun. Koko likes to take risks and does not often think or care about the consequences that may follow. He often looks like a "wild thing" from Maurice Sendak's book *Where the Wild Things Are.* Koko expresses his feelings in very loud and big ways, which sometimes gets him into trouble. He is often distracted and not able to sit still. The feelings he shows are limited to big happy and big mad; it is difficult for him to express his sad or scared feelings. When something upsets him he will act out and appear angry. Koko does not understand how Bunny can "do nothing" and often tries to solicit Bunny into acting more like him.

The adults in his life are confused by his behaviors and often believe he just likes to get negative attention. Unfortunately, he does not know how to ask for what he wants, and he does not understand what many of his feelings are or how to express them appropriately. By attending the group and participating in the activities with Bunny and the children, he learns how to use his words and express some of his thoughts and emotions. The group leaders and Max/Maxine help him understand some of the events that have happened in his family and how his thoughts and reactions to them are similar to others who have been in those situations. By the end of the program, thanks to assistance from the group members, especially Max/Maxine, Koko has learned how to control his internal "wild thing" and appropriately express a full range of emotions.

It is important for the group leaders, the children in the group, Koko's adults, and most important Koko himself to understand that he is not "bad." He and the participants in the group program are taught that feelings are not right or wrong, but there are ways to express them that are okay and not okay. The people in Koko's life do not understand why he behaves the way he does and how he is reacting to the traumas he has experienced in his life. Like Koko, many children who have witnessed or experienced trauma in their lives have learned how to survive in this environment. They can relate to Koko, and by watching him and helping him learn new skills they are learning better ways to express themselves as well. Koko is exuberant and caring. Although he is known for his naughtiness, he is not unkind or cruel.

Bunny

Although the book refers to Bunny as "she" and "her," it would be inappropriate for her to be always thought of or labeled as a girl. Her experiences and ways of coping are common for both boys and girls, and they all can relate to and learn with her.

Bunny is a shy and timid rabbit who does not like to take risks or get into trouble. She is very cautious and careful, always watching what is going on around her. Unlike Koko, Bunny wants to please the adults and works hard to follow the rules and not do anything wrong. Loud noises, yelling, and fighting upset her; she will run and hide if she senses any conflict or problem around her. Koko calls Bunny "boring" and believes she does not want to have fun.

Bunny will tell you that she is feeling happy or fine; she does not like to feel mad or sad. Any feelings Bunny does have are very small. She does not want to bother the people around her and often does not feel entitled to have her own feelings or to express them to others. Instead, Bunny will keep her feelings inside, which causes her to have somatic symptoms such as headaches or stomachaches. She does not understand that holding her feelings in leads to her body not feeling well. She often rubs her stomach, holds her head down, or curls up and tries to make herself invisible.

The adults in Bunny's life do not believe or understand that she is having any problems at all. She is well behaved, does not get into trouble at school or home, and tries hard to be quiet and do what she is told. The adults have not made the connection between her somatic complaints and her inability to express her feelings. Bunny and her adults need to be taught that she has feelings inside that she is not letting out, that all is not fine, as she initially portrays.

The group is a place for Bunny to learn that she has feelings and that there are appropriate ways for them to be expressed. She starts to find that when she lets her feelings out, even in small ways, that nothing bad happens. In fact, she starts to feel better when she does this! As Bunny becomes more assertive by participating in the activities in the group, those around her start to notice the changes. Koko is very happy with the differences he notices in Bunny and cheers her on. The adults, however, are not always pleased with what they see. Bunny starts to speak up as the weeks progress and say what she is feeling about past and present events. Bunny's family and teachers are not used to this Bunny, who is beginning to have a range of feelings and words to express herself.

Like Bunny, many children who have witnessed or experienced trauma in their lives have learned how to survive in this kind of environment by making themselves "invisible." They hide themselves and their feelings and focus solely on the environment and the people in it. By teaching Bunny about feelings and how to express them appropriately, they too learn that it can feel good to do this. The adults who live with and take care of Bunny and children like her also need to be educated about the changes they see, and how they can see these as positive behaviors and learn to reinforce them. Bunny is kind and gentle. Although she is known for being a "good bunny" she is just like any other child who wants to play and have fun.

GROUP STRUCTURE AND HANDLING BEHAVIORS

Each week, group begins with the leaders and children sitting in a circle or around a table. Bunny and Koko should always be visible, if not worn by the group leaders. The children will ask about them and become anxious if they cannot see them, as the puppets soon become viewed as members of the group.

Group always starts with check-in. Each child is encouraged to participate. It can be helpful to have paper and markers or crayons out for the children to use during this time. Although it can be somewhat distracting, being able to color does keep the children focused, and it is a way for some to contain their anxiety.

If the activities from any session are not completed in a week, they can be carried over to the next week. It is difficult to predict which activities any particular group of children will need more time with or speed through quickly.

Enlarged photocopies of the drawings included at the end of some of the sessions can be used most any week, integrated into the curriculum as the group leaders find appropriate. The children enjoy coloring them in, and they should each be asked to tell a story about what is happening in the picture. This can be diagnostic, and it usually leads to interesting and useful discussions in the group. Some pictures may not be applicable to some groups of children or may be too stimulating or anxiety producing. The leaders should use their clinical judgment.

Group should end each week with snack. Approximately ten minutes should be left at the end of each session to serve it and do some closure activities. The leaders may find it useful to keep a supply of picture books or poems to read to the children during snack time, before or after they have been asked to share what they liked and did not like about group that day. The children naturally calm down during story time and will generally settle in to eat and listen as a leader reads to them. It is helpful to put the drawing materials back out during this time as well.

Snacks and Snack Time

The children will probably ask for snack throughout group, especially if the material is uncomfortable. Snacks are served only at snack time, which is usually about ten minutes before group ends. Be sure you allow enough time for snack; if it is too long, they get anxious and focus on wanting more, and if it is too short, they feel rushed and anxious about not getting enough.

The rules are two snacks per child and as much drink as they need. These rules are necessary because food is usually a big issue for the children in these groups. The children may need reminders that snacks are for eating in the group. Some children will try to save snack to feed to family members later. This perpetuates their roles in, and the dynamics of, their families, which is not healthy for the children.

Group members may also try to hoard snacks, saying they did not have seconds when it is actually in their pockets. It is important for the group leaders to communicate with each other about who has been served what, to avoid this happening. One leader can say to the other, "Oh, he's already had two snacks today." The second leader can respond, "Oops, okay. I understand you're hungry, but you've had your two snacks for today."

When Disruptive Behavior Occurs

The material is designed to elicit memories and feelings that are sometimes difficult for the children. They often respond by not responding or by talking too much. No child should be forced to answer or participate in any activity. Children often know their own comfort levels and will do what they can do on any particular day. Children still benefit from the material even though they are not directly engaged in the activity. Encourage any appropriate participation with verbal reinforcements. If the child does not draw in an activity, ask her or him what she or he would have drawn, when the children are sharing their drawings.

Sometimes a child behaves like a "wild thing" even when the group is not doing a role-play. Please remember that this child is not out of control. This is the child's way of coping with the material being presented, with the feelings that are coming up, and with the world in general. This child is usually trying her or his best to behave. The child has gotten the message from many sources that she or he is "bad" or "naughty," and is expecting to get the same message from the group leader. It is important not to perpetuate this idea, but instead, teach the child a different way to cope. This child can be redirected with comments from the leader such as, "I can't hear you right now; Joe is talking." If the leader sits next to this child or between him or her and the peer he or she is talking to the most, this can help decrease the disruptive behavior. Comment to the child, "I like the way you're listening" or give other positive feedback to reinforce this behavior. The group leader reminds the children that snack cannot be served until people are sitting down in their chairs.

Time-Out

A helpful behavior management technique is time-out. A time-out is not a punishment. It is an opportunity to stop a child before his or her behavior escalates. It is usually thirty seconds to a minute outside the room *with a group leader,* away from the stimulation of the group. The leader does not talk to the child until the time-out is over. Then, the leader asks the child, "How come you got/wanted time out?" and "Are you ready to go back in group?" This is not a time to process what happened that day or what is going on the child's family life. The goal is for the child to rejoin group as soon as possible.

The time-out is introduced when the leader finds the child unable to use verbal redirection. The leader should ask the child, "Can you stop yourself, or do you need time-out?" If the answer is 'yes' to the second question the child has time-out, no matter how much they protest. Otherwise, the leader is likely to end up in a power struggle with the child.

Tokens or Rewards

Items such as stickers, Skittles, or gummy candies are given to the children during the end of group, after they have responded to the questions about what they liked and did not like about group that day. These items are transitional objects, things the children can take with them out of the group. It is also helpful to use tokens or rewards during other times in group to get the children refocused or ready for participating in a particular activity. A group leader may say, "Everybody can earn a sticker if they are trying to draw a picture of their family." Another possibility is, "The group is getting so loud! Anyone using an inside voice can earn a Skittle." The idea is for each child to be able to earn a token or reward, so everyone feels included and special. No one should be singled out to earn or not earn something.

Coleading the Little Kids' Group

With this population especially, it is very important that the two leaders of the group are in communication with each other continually. Process comments made out loud to each other are an effective way to redirect the group, notice a theme, or relieve some of the children's anxiety. For example, one leader may say to the other, "It's hard for the group to talk about feelings today." Group leaders need to be validating the group as a whole, not so much individual kids. A leader could say, "Wow, the group is doing such a good job working on their drawings."

Because the material can be provocative, some children react by distancing themselves from the group or acting out. One group leader can say to the other, "It can be tough to talk about family." This validates the children's experience and relieves some anxiety. It also encourages a sense of safety, which benefits the whole group.

The two leaders need to be in agreement about how behaviors are handled. These children are good at getting what they want, and their choices are often uncomfortable for adults. It's important to be flexible and to expect and allow the children to use their own coping mechanisms. This may involve ignoring a child who is wiggling or not sitting in his or her chair; this child is very likely listening to everything and trying to assimilate the information the best that he or she can.

PART II:
BIG KIDS' (BK) MANUAL

BK Session 1

Saying Hello and Making a Safe Place to Work Together

Goals

To create common ground and safety

To provide pleasurable opportunities to use peers to help cope with interpersonal problems

To help children identify a range of feelings that they may have experienced in response to loss, change, family violence, or conflict

Note: Save all work generated during the group. Be sure that it is clearly labeled. Keep each child's work in a separate folder that can be reviewed with the child in an individual follow-up session and selectively with parents when the child permits.

Materials

Note: Materials starred with an asterisk (*) are reproduced in the manual at the end of the session.

Polaroid camera and film or digital camera (optional)

Folder for each child in the group

3x5 cards folded in half

Plenty of paper, pencils, markers, and rulers

A poster board for rules (See Section C of this session; after it is made, display this chart in every session.)

Large sheets of blank paper

*List of feelings

Procedure

Clinical note: Emphasis is on creating a sense of common ground and safety.

A. Introduction

Each week, when the children arrive, they are asked to sit in a circle or around a table. This is a ritual for the beginning (and ending) of each week's group, though many of the activities require a less formal approach. The leaders introduce themselves and discuss the purpose of group.

It can be interesting to ask the children if they know or if someone explained to them why they have come today. The older children may say that they "had" to come or "the court made me." School-age children are more likely to attribute their attendance to parental divorce or their "family problems." The group leader validates their input, then clarifies the purpose of the group by saying something such as:

> I'm so glad you all were able to come today. I'm really looking forward to us getting to know one another, doing some work, as well as having some fun together. In case you didn't know, I'd like to tell you right away that all of you share something in common. You have all had some difficult times in your families. Some of you have had experience with fighting in your families, which can be frightening and hard to live with. Some of you are missing people who don't live in your family anymore. [Add if appropriate] Some of you have parents who live apart, and some of you do not. [Or add if appropriate] You also all have parents who don't live together because they are separated or divorced.

It is important to allow the children some time to respond to the leader's statements. A few of them will probably want to share experiences or events that have occurred in their families. Some may not; although the leader can ask a child if he or she would like to say something, no one should be forced to share if he or she is not ready to.

B. Warm-Up

After introducing himself or herself, the leader goes around the table in order and asks each child to say his or her name and something else that is nonthreatening and fun. The leader may say: "Please tell your name and what food you absolutely won't eat!" or "What is your name and what is your favorite TV show?" This question can be anything that is friendly and easy to talk about. This is a way to ease the tension of the first meeting and find common ground among group members. The leader then hands each child a 3x5 card or manila folders cut into fourths and asks the children to write their names on them, encouraging them to color or decorate them as they wish. While they are doing this, the leader says:

> Everyone has something that makes them different than the other people in their family. Maybe you are great at skateboarding, but no one else in your family likes to do this. Maybe you won't eat pepperoni pizza but your whole family likes to order this when you go out. Think about how you are different from the rest of your family. Anyone have any ideas?

When the children start responding, the group leader can clarify what they say. For example, a child raises her or his hand and says, "I like horses." The leader asks if anyone else likes them, and the child responds that her or his brother does, "sort of." The leader can support the child by noting that because she or he likes horses more than anyone else in her or his family, that's one of the ways she or he is different from them.

The children are then asked to write or draw their responses to this question on the card or paper they are using for their name tags.

If a Polaroid or digital camera is available, the leader can take a picture of each child and attach it to the name card. Only the group leader should use the camera, and no additional pictures should be taken of the children, individually or in groups.

The leader then says in his or her own words:

> At the end of group, I will collect the name tags you made today. I will set them out at the beginning of group next time. That will mark your place to sit in group. It will stay the same for the

whole time. If you are absent, we will have your name tag to keep your special place.

The leader who has had individual intake sessions with all the children can comment in his or her own words:

I have met you all separately, and you and I have shared some things about your family situation that you may or may not want to share with the group. That's your decision to make.

The leader then continues in his or her own words, regarding confidentiality:

If something comes up during the group and any of you find you'd like to talk with me privately, please let me know. Please don't talk to other kids about what goes on here. It's important for us all to feel safe and private, so that we can tell what we want to tell and keep things private when we want to. It is up to you, though, whether you talk to your parents about group. As most of you know, I will be working with your parents also. I will try to help them understand you, but I will not tell them exact things you say or show them any work you do without your permission.

We will be meeting every week for the next [Specify number] weeks. We will all be here to help one another. Each time we meet we will do four things:

1. We will do some relaxation exercises to help us get calmed down.
2. We will do an activity to get to know one another and ourselves better.
3. We will do some role-playing, which we will videotape.
4. We will watch ourselves on video and eat a snack.

You will each have a chance to be in charge of the role-plays and to watch others role-playing as well. Everyone will also have a turn to be the cameraperson. Let's decide now on the order for taking turns as cameraperson.

The leader helps group determine a sequence for camera duty that gives a fair share of time to each group member, then asks for questions and points of clarification and generally checks in with the group to reflect and clarify feelings that children may be communicating nonverbally. The leader may then wish to model identification and expression of feelings by sharing his or her own feelings about the group.

C. Rules (To Be Posted at Each Session)

Clinical note: Emphasis is on communicating real concern for the children's sense of safety in the group. For this reason it is important for the leader, not the children, to take responsibility for the following tasks.

The leader says in his or her own words: "Let's think of three or four simple rules for the group that will help us all feel safe."

The leader encourages the children to come up with and agree on rules. If necessary, the leader facilitates by suggesting the following rules. The group should end up with some variant of these rules plus one or two additional rules. The leader writes them on the chart. This chart will be displayed at every session.

1. Only one person speaks at a time.
2. Listen when another person is talking.
3. No gossiping outside of group (that includes the leader).
4. No put-downs.

D. The House My Family Lives In

Clinical note: Emphasis is on identifying similarities that create common ground as well as supporting differences in feelings and family structures.

The leader says in his or her own words:

> Now that we have some rules, let's take some time to show one another the different people in our family and where they live. Think first about the people that are part of your family. You might want to include your mother, father, brothers, sisters, grandparents, or special friends. Remember, group is a safe

place for you and your ideas. There may be people who are not really in your family, but you think of them as family, so you can include them if you like. There might be other people who think they're in your family, but you don't feel that way about them, so you can leave them out or draw them on the back if you like. Then think about where everyone lives.

The leader may model by drawing the houses or apartments where members of his or her immediate or extended family live. Group members begin working as soon as they understand the task. Very anxious/vigilant children may wish to use rulers. Some children will turn to their peers to help them draw or to do the task for them. It is important to encourage them to do their own work and to reassure them that it is their effort that is important. After the drawings are finished, each child may share his or her drawing and name family members. The leader follows each child's presentation with one or two of these questions:

> Do you go back and forth between your mother's and your father's houses, or between their fights at home?
> Is that difficult?
> What is difficult about that?
> What is fun about that?
> Do you ever wish you could live with someone else or spend more time with someone else in your family?
> Do you sometimes wish that someone in your family was not there? (or) Who would you like to have in your family?

The following additional questions are for younger children only.

> Is someone still in your family if they go and live in a different house?
> Can you love someone who lives in a different house just as much as someone who lives with you?

E. List of Feelings

Clinical note: The emphasis is on helping the children to identify as wide a range of feelings as possible and creating and encouraging an accepting atmosphere. It is important to include the concept of mixed and complex feelings as well as the more basic feelings. The leader should take the responsibility for writing out the feeling list.

The leader provides some type of verbal transition and closure from the previous activity, then says in his or her own words:

> I'd like us to do something together that other groups have done with me before. We all had a lot of fun. What we did was to make a list of all the different feelings that group members had about the fighting and arguing that has gone on in their families. Kids came up with all kinds of feelings—mad, bad, sad, scared, and so on. I have an old list here from a group I had before. I'd like us to make our own list together, and we'll see if you can get as many feelings on your list as there are on my old list. Maybe you can get even more. I'll write, and you can just tell me what to put on our list.

As the list is compiled, the leader continually encourages a wide range of feelings and the possibility of outdoing the old list (see List of Feelings, p. 109). When the new list is done, the group compares lists. Children like to count the number of feelings in the old list and the new list. When the counting is done, compare. Children can add from the old list to their list as well as cross out items on the old list that they do not like. When the comparing, adding, and crossing out are done, the leader creates some closure by commenting on the range of feelings and noting how some feelings are easier to talk about than others, how feelings vary from time to time, and how feelings mix together.

F. Feelings/Color

In this activity, the leader helps the children to create a color-coded chart on which the identified feelings are associated with a particular color or combination of colors. For example, "angry" may be red, whereas "embarrassed" may be red combined with other colors because it has an anger component. Other colors in the combination should reflect the other feeling components. The group should decide on each color or color combination by consensus as much as possible. The leader should decide, if there is disagreement. Once the color or color combination is chosen, the feeling word should be circled in that color or combination of colors on the feelings chart. It is not necessary to spend huge amounts of time on each decision. The finished chart is the point. It will be a useful tool in future sessions.

G. Closure, Snack, and Housekeeping

Clinical note: The emphasis is on creating a sense of order, continuity, and safekeeping. Again, the leader takes the responsibility for the following tasks and does not assign them to the children or allow them to volunteer. It is important for the children to experience caretaking and nurturing by an adult, since many of them are prone to role reversal and taking care of others.

At the end of the group session, with about ten minutes left, the children are asked to sit down in a circle or around the table, similar to the way group began. The leader collects name tags, stressing that they will be put out at the next group meeting. The leader collects any artwork that the children have done and makes sure that the work has their names on it. The leader places the work in each child's folder and reassures the group that their work will be kept safely for them until next time.

The group leader shows the children the choices for snack and asks each child what she or he would like. It's important that the adult serves the snack to each child, for reasons of hygiene as well as to decrease favoritism and possible conflicts between members. The leader reviews the rules for snack, which may include the following:

1. State how many servings are allowed each week (this remains constant).
2. Snacks are for yourself and not for sharing.
3. Snacks are to be eaten in the room and not saved for later.

During snack, this and each week, the group leader asks each member to share one thing she or he liked and did not like about the group today. Some responses may be as general as "nothing" or "everything" as answers to either or both questions. This is acceptable, though the leader may want to offer praise to those children who elaborate on their answers. Also during this time, the leader reviews the name of the cameraperson for next week and reminds that child to come fifteen minutes early to practice with the video camera.

List of Feelings: Materials for Session 1

Happy	Excited
Angry	Mad
Frustrated	Upset
Calm	Relaxed
Proud	Pleased
Depressed	Hateful
Hated	Shy
Afraid	Pressured
Worried	Confused
Loved	Liked
Warm	Comfortable
Safe	Private
Sad	Left out
Fidgety	Guilty
Jealous	Scared
Helpless	Embarrassed
Joyful	Amused

Exploring Levels of Feelings, Actions, and Points of View

Goals

To create common ground and safety

To help the children to become aware that feelings can be experienced at different levels of intensity

To help the children to understand the difference between feelings and actions

To introduce the idea of right and wrong ways to act on feelings

To help the children to define their own perspectives on family conflict

Materials

Note: Materials starred with an asterisk (*) are reproduced in the manual at the end of the session.

Video camera and monitor

Rules chart (posted in group room)

Feelings/color chart developed in Session 1 (posted in group room)

Name tags and folders (to be kept in leader's possession and placed around the table before each session)

Plenty of paper, pencils, markers, and rulers

Blindfold

*Feelings measure chart

*Shoe box (or larger box)

Procedure

A. Warm-Up

When the group is seated in a circle or around a table, the leader makes a brief statement of welcome. Then the group begins with check-in, which involves asking each child to say something about his or her day and choose a feeling word to describe how he or she is feeling at that time. The children are encouraged to use words from the list created last week or to use one of their own, which can then be added to the list if the group or leader wishes. Some will answer easily and are pleased to be asked, while others are more reticent and require some encouragement. For the child who says "fine," the group leader may say something such as: "Hmm . . . I don't see that word on our list. Is there anything up there that is close to how you're feeling today?" Some children will still be stuck, having little or no practice thinking about or verbalizing their feelings. To support them, a leader can say: "Well, think about the five main feelings: happy, mad, sad, scared, and surprised. Are any of these sort of what you're feeling?"

This will usually help a child begin to understand, and she or he will probably say, "Well, I guess sort of _____." If the child is still shrugging her or his shoulders and saying "I dunno," the group leader will still thank her or him for trying.

When each child shares a feeling word, the leader asks for an explanation about why she or he is feeling that way today, saying something such as: "Can you tell us why you feel 'sort of mad' today?" Again, if the child cannot explain why, the leader does not insist on a response but accepts this and moves on.

The leader reminds the children who the cameraperson is according to the sequence determined during closure in Session 1. The leader briefly reviews the rules that were agreed upon in Session 1 and listed on the posted chart.

Note on timing: The following activity can take up most of the session. The leader can solve this problem by using the same obstacle course for each blind walker and using a timer with a loud bell. The leader then allocates three to five minutes per blind walker. When the bell goes off, the course ends wherever the blind walker happens to be.

B. Blind Walk

Clinical note: The goal is to create trust within the group and allow children to experience some dependency on peers. It is vital that the walk be conducted safely. The leader should point out how important it is to be able to receive help from friends and how good it can feel. Each guide and blindfolded follower should be applauded when they reach "home" or the end of their allotted time. Each should be complimented, one for being such a good caretaker and the other for taking a chance and being brave.

For the Blind Walk activity, the group is directed to create an obstacle course though which each group member will be guided while blindfolded.

1. A volunteer is identified (or selected) and blindfolded. (Reassurance from the leader here is both necessary and appropriate.)
2. Each group member is then given a portion of the obstacle course to supervise and is responsible for guiding the blindfolded child safely through his or her part of the obstacle course, either by giving verbal directions or by leading the blindfolded child by hand. (For older children or mixed-gender groups, verbal directions may have to replace physical contact between group members.)
3. The leader oversees the course to make sure it is connected and safe. If there is time, the obstacles in the course are changed after each blind walker is identified and blindfolded. The process is repeated until each group member has gone through the course blindfolded.

C. Level of Feelings

Clinical note: The focus of this exercise is to make feelings seem less uncontrollable by introducing the idea that feelings may be experienced at different levels rather than in all-or-nothing extremes.

The leader passes out copies of the feelings measure chart (see Materials section) to each child and goes over the feelings that are labeled under the first three measures. The leader explains that other children whose parents are fighting, separated, or divorced sometimes have these feelings. The leader asks the children to fill in how strongly they have felt these three feelings in their own lives. The leader says in his or her own words:

> Now pick two, three, or four other feelings that are most true for you and write them in under the other four measures on your chart. You can use the feelings/color chart to help you if you like. After you have filled in the name of each feeling, decide how strongly you feel this way and fill that in too.

When the exercise is completed, the leader invites each group member to share what he or she has done. Prompt questions about feelings should be selected by the leader from the following:

> What do you usually do when you feel [fill in a feeling]?
> Do you ever feel_____in a different amount?
> What do you do then and how is that different?
> What makes you feel_____?
> When you feel extremely_____, what can make you feel different?
> How about when you feel just a little_____?

D. Charade of Feelings

Clinical note: This activity introduces role-playing and the idea that different levels of feelings are acted on in different ways. Again, the point is to make feelings seem less uncontrollable. This is also the time that different perspectives are introduced and differentiated. This is done by acting out the feeling (first-person perspective), guessing what the feeling is (second-person perspective), and by video recording the charades and playing them back to the children during snack time at the end of the session (third-person perspective).

The leader says in her or his own words: "Now that we have had a chance to talk about feelings a little, I would like to get ready to do some role-playing. We'll start with charades. Who can tell me what charades are?"

Seek and summarize the children's response. Then the leader says in her or his own words:

Okay, let's start out simply. The charades will help us to role-play our feelings and think about how people might show a little bit of a feeling instead of a lot of that feeling. I would like each of you to pick one feeling from your chart and then get ready to charade the feeling. It will be our job to guess the feeling and how much you are feeling it. The cameraperson will video the charade.

The leader goes around the table giving each group member a turn. Passing is okay, but the leader should gently press by saying, for example: "Could you charade a person sleeping or feeling nothing? Would that be okay?"

Note: It is very important to go gently and respectfully, being alert to the need to back off quickly if the child is obviously uncomfortable.

Go around the table once or twice, as long as the group is focused.

E. Points of View

Note on timing: There may be very little time left for this activity after the Blind Walk. This activity requires at least twenty minutes. If there is not enough time to complete it in this session, introduce it in Session 3, after the fantasy and relaxation exercises.

Clinical note: The focus of this activity is to help the children to gain some distance and perspective on the family conflict.

For the Points of View activity, a shoe box (see Materials section) is placed in the center of the group table in such a way that only the black side can be seen from one side of the room, only the white side can be seen from the opposite side of the room, and the black, gray, and white sides can be seen only from the adjacent sides. The leader may need to raise the box (put it on books, etc.) in order to achieve these perspectives. The leader says in his or her own words: "Let's do something with this box. Believe it or not, this box is going to help us understand a bit about grown-up fights. Let's do a little role-play using this box."

The leader selects or asks for three volunteers, one for "Mom" one for "Dad" and one for "Child" (both boys and girls may play any of these three roles if they are comfortable doing so). The other group members will have the job of watching the role-play and giving advice to Child. The leader directs Dad to stand on one side of the table (so he can see only the black side of the box). Mom is to stand on the opposite side of the table (so she can see only the white side of the box), and Child is to stand on the adjacent side (where he or she can see the tri-colored side). The leader then asks Dad to describe what he sees to Mom. Focus on eliciting the color. Prompts include: "How do you feel? A lot or a little?"

Then the leader asks Mom to describe what she sees to Dad. Focus on eliciting the color.

> How does Mom feel now? How much?
> How does Dad feel now? How much?
> How is Child beginning to feel?

The leader facilitates the exercise as it becomes a fight over black and white. Prompts include eliciting feelings of all players as the fight escalates. Child's role is to observe. In this exercise it is important to rotate players from position to position, eliciting and noticing changes in feelings as points of view change. Prompts include:

> How did you feel as Dad (as Mom, as Child)?
> How did your feelings change when you saw the gray side?

Changes could be in feelings or degree of feeling. After the fight has escalated and both parents are very angry, leader elicits from Child what he or she sees.

> What do you see?
> Why can't Mom see what you see?
> Why can't Dad see what you see?
> What is this like for you?

Clinical note: Here the focus is on helping the child to see that there is some black (Dad is partly right), some white (Mom is partly right), and some gray (both right, both wrong).

The leader says in her or his own words:

> When you see both sides, it's very confusing and frustrating! Some kids find it easier to see only black or only white. Other

kids prefer not to look at all. What can kids do in a situation like this?

Discussion should emphasize that parents will not see things differently if they do not want to; it is not possible for the child to make them move or see differently, so the child's choices are (try to elicit from observers):

- Keep trying to move them. (Leader notes that this can be exhausting, impossible, too hard.)
- Understand there is no solution. They can argue about black and white forever.
- Child can try to figure out who's right and who's wrong. Notice that both are right, but both are failing to see the gray, so don't waste too much time on figuring it out.
- Child can stay and watch and worry, or try to figure it out. (Leader notes that this can be exhausting and that it takes up lots of time.)
- Leader elicits other age-appropriate activities from group—such as roller skating, homework, biking, reading—that Child could be spending time on.

If time permits, all group members should participate and rotate at least once.

F. Closure, Snack, and Housekeeping

The closing ritual of the group occurs now, as described in the previous week's session, and will continue thus at the end of each group. The children are asked to sit down around the table or in the original circle to get ready for the end of group. The leader asks each child what she or he wants, then distributes the snack and has group members label and put away any drawings, name cards, etc. While they are eating, the leader has the option of replaying the video of the charades (without the sound) and the children are invited to identify the feelings that were being expressed in the video and what made them think so. Finally, the leader asks the children to share something they liked and did not like about the group session today, then reviews the name of the cameraperson for next week and reminds that child to come fifteen minutes early.

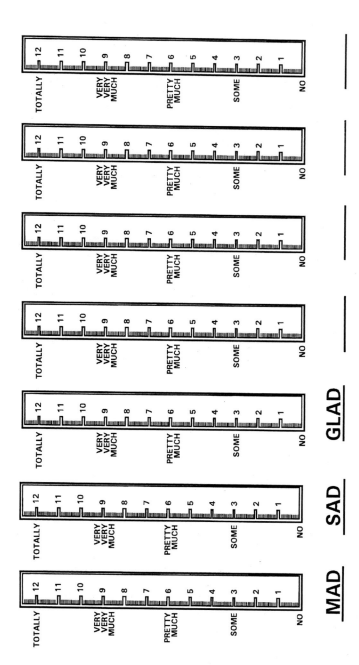

Materials needed:
Black, grey, and white paper
Scissors
Box
Glue

1. Cover top of box starting on the left side with grey paper so that the grey paper hangs over the left and right side of box and glue down on to the box.

1.

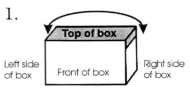

Left side of box   Front of box   Right side of box

2. Cover front of box starting at the bottom and overlap grey paper on top of box about 1/3 in from top front edge.

2.

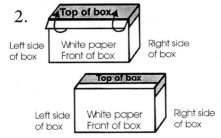

3. Cover back of box starting at the bottom and overlap grey paper on top of box about 1/3 in from top back edge.

3.

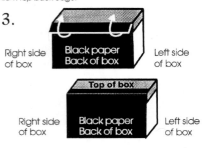

4.

Finished Box

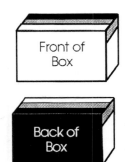

BK Session 3

Making a Safe Inside Place and Learning the Rules of Role-Play

Goals

To help the children to define and understand themselves by introducing the idea of a safe inner space

To teach the way role-playing will be done in group

To help the children to dramatize their own experience of being
caught in the family conflict so their thoughts and feelings
can be identified, fantasies and wishes can be clarified and reality tested, and issues of right and wrong can be discussed

Materials

Note: Materials starred with an asterisk (*) are reproduced in the
manual at the end of the session.

Video camera and monitor

Rules chart (posted in group room)

Feelings/color chart developed in Session 1 (posted in group
room)

Name tags and folders (to be kept in leader's possession)

Plenty of paper, pencils, markers, and rulers

*Picture of child caught between two parents *or* picture of father
leaving mother and child

Procedure

A. Warm-Up

When the group is seated in a circle or around a table, the leader makes a brief statement of welcome. Then the group begins with check-in, which involves asking each child to say something about her or his day and choose a feeling word to describe how she or he is feeling. The children are encouraged to use words from the list or to use one of their own, which can then be added to the list if the group or leader wishes.

B. Relaxation

The idea of relaxation and calming oneself is introduced to the children. A group leader may use the "smell the cookies, blow out the candles" exercise (for younger children):

> Let's try something. Sit up and put your hands on your tummies. (If the group leader models this, the children are more likely to follow along.) Think of something that smells really good, like cookies. I'd like you to pretend you're smelling cookies, and breathe in through your nose. Then, pretend you're blowing out candles, and blow the air out through your mouth. Ready? Okay, let's all practice.

The leader, who also participates, encourages all the children to do this approximately three times. To continue the lesson, the leader asks the members to think of other things that smell good. For example: "Sally suggested pizza. Yum, that does smell good. Okay, everyone smell the pizza . . . now blow on it to cool it off."

Alternatively, a "countdown" relaxation exercise can be introduced (for older children), in which the children are encouraged to tighten and hunch up their shoulders, stomachs, arms, and legs tightly and then progressively relax while the leader counts down from ten to zero.

It helps the children to understand why they are being asked to do these exercises. The leader may say:

This is a great way to get calm. Breathing this way slows your body down and can help you if you're trying to fall asleep or need to get ready to take a test in school. When else could you use this technique?

C. A Fantasy Room

Clinical note: This exercise is a concrete way to help the children to think about themselves and their boundaries. The room that is created will be used in subsequent sessions to help the children visualize a private, soothing place to be in during relaxation exercises.

The leader says a brief word of welcome to the group in general and acknowledges each child individually while distributing name tags and noting who will be the cameraperson today. The leader says in his or her own words:

> Today we're going to spend about ten minutes on ourselves. Let me tell you why I think it's important to do this. Sometimes when families/parents fight, I have noticed that kids spend a lot of time thinking about the fighting. Some kids worry about it.

The leader makes reference here to the feelings/color chart: "As you see from this list, other kids feel [Fill in with feelings that suggest worry or avoidance]." The leader notes ways in which such feelings focus children's attention away from their own needs, and says in his or her own words:

> Now it does seem that that's a lot of work, and it makes it difficult, sometimes, to think about who you are as a x-year-old person: what you think, what you feel, what you like and don't like. So in this session, let's just take about ten minutes to think about these things. I'm going to give you some paper, and I want you to have fun drawing your very own room. No one may enter this room but you, unless you decide to invite someone in. No one at all. It is completely your own.

The leader distributes drawing paper and continues:

> You can draw your room with or without a lock, with or without windows. It can be large or small. Underground, aboveground, or in the sky. It can be any color and, best of all, it can have anything in it you like. Anything at all. Go as far as your imagination will carry you.

While the group is working, the leader comments supportively about each drawing and asks the children to try to stay relaxed. The leader allows about ten minutes for this activity, then brings the activity to a close and asks group members if they would like to share their drawings.

D. Rules of Role-Play

Clinical note: The emphasis is on empowering the child director as author of her or his own history and destiny, helping children become aware that different feelings are associated with different roles, that some feelings are easily shown while others are not, and that feelings vary in level or intensity. However, children should not be left with the image of the violence or the trauma that initially occurred, which is then reenacted in their role-play. It is imperative that the leader makes sure there is time for the child, with the help of the group, to "rewrite" the script of the story, so that the children can redo the role-play with a more appropriate, safer ending.

The leader is now ready to introduce role-playing, which will be conducted according to the following rules. The leader should review these rules prior to the group and then paraphrase them to the group members at this time.

1. Ideas for role-plays come from the children whenever possible.
2. The child who makes up the role-play has the choice of being the director. The director picks who plays what role, reminds the group of the story, and directs what they say, how they say it, and what movement is appropriate. The leader facilitates and supports the director. It is important, before the role-play begins, to help the director to identify a feeling for each role and how the feeling is to be shown or hidden. The possibility of mixed or ambivalent feelings should be suggested when appropriate and whenever possible.

3. If the child who offers the role-play chooses not to be the director, he or she may select a role to play and may choose another director.
4. Children may negotiate for a different role when picked or, if the child prefers no role, he or she is included in the role of houseplant, family pet, etc. This is true even for the child who offered the role-play. This way no child stays completely out of the role-play.
5. All role-plays are videotaped by the cameraperson for the week. Videotapes are reviewed at the end of the session.
6. In any story where violence is re-created, the children should be reminded that this is pretend, not real, and that no hitting or hands on each other can occur.
7. In theory, all group members should have a chance to take each role. In practice, the group will probably get to do the role-play about three times, with different children in different roles each time.

E. Role-Play of Child Caught Between Parents
or *Father Leaving Mother and Child*

Clinical note: The focus is on helping the child to identify the feelings she or he has when caught in the middle, differentiate these feelings from the feelings of the parents in the conflict situation, identify fantasies and wishes, and engage in reality testing.

The leader shows the picture of a child caught between two parents or the picture of a father leaving a mother and child (see pages 126 and 127) to the group and initiates a discussion by asking the groups questions such as:

> What is happening here?
> What do you think the child is feeling?
> What do you think each adult is feeling?
> Did anything like this ever happen to you or someone else that you know?

The children are invited to color the picture and maybe to draw a little cartoon bubble for the words that are being said in the picture. The leader may say:

> Think about where it happened, who said what, etc. Then take the colored markers and color all the feelings each one has in the

picture. You can color little balloons with the words inside, floating over the person like in a cartoon drawing and using the feelings/color chart as a guide.

The leader asks if one of the children who self-discloses would like to direct a role-play. Work proceeds according to the rules described previously. During and/or after each role-play the leader should help the role-players to generate as many different feelings as possible. The leader gives lots of encouragement for discriminating between feelings, differentiating people's feelings, and discriminating levels of feeling. The leader may model responses. If children have difficulty in identifying feelings, use the feelings/color chart as a prompt. Also, the leader helps children to discriminate how much of each feeling they have in the role-play (totally, pretty much, etc.), as on the feelings measure chart from Session 2. Leader must restore the child's "face" if she or he reveals weakness, pain, or embarrassment. The leader may say, for example: "[Child's name] was really very brave/very honest, when she [he] said [Quote the child]." Then it is useful to point out the "no-win" situation: "Sometimes, if you obey your mom, you disobey your dad (and vice versa)."

Clinical note: Validate all feelings. Emphasize that feelings are never wrong, that it's what you do with feelings in action that can be right or wrong, and that different people can have different or similar feelings about the same event (using differences among group members as examples). This will help counter the feelings of helplessness, blame, shame, etc.

The leader can encourage fantasies of what the children would like to have happened during the role-play. For example, at the end of a role-play, the leader can say in his or her own words: "How would you like to have intervened/acted? Pretend that you are all-powerful or magic; what would you do? Let's do the role-play that way." During and after the role-play, the leader notes the realities of the situation and the constraints on the children. The leader says in his or her own words:

> Do you think [the fantasy] might happen? No! I agree, it won't. [If the child has expressed fears, add the following] It was a good idea not to say anything. You were afraid you'd only make them madder if you did.

The leader validates that they were in a very difficult situation and that they were very brave or wise or did all they could at the time. The leader may point out that it is unfair to children when they are put in these situations.

Clinical note: During this and subsequent weeks' video reviews, the group leader will want to introduce at appropriate opportunities ways that the children can keep themselves safe. A discussion of safety planning can be generated and revisited throughout the following sessions. Specifically, the children are invited to come up with a list of ways they can keep themselves safe, and this can be maintained as another list in the group room that is added to each week.

F. Video Review and Snack

For the closing ritual, the children are asked to sit around the table or in the original circle to get ready to end the group. The leader asks each child what she or he wants, then distributes the snack. After the children have their snacks in hand, the videotaped role-plays are reviewed. Again, emphasis is on eliciting the feelings of the child and differentiating them from the feelings of the parents in the conflict situation. The children become anxious if they are not allowed to watch the tape of the day's role-plays through once without interruption. Thus, the leader needs to allow them to see this, rewind the tape (just today's video), and then stop it as the scenes occur that she or he wants to discuss or look at more closely. Closure questions from the leader to the group at this time include the following points:

> Do you think what is happening is fair?
> What do the parents want the child to do?
> What does the child wish he/she could do?
> What can a child do (to keep safe)?
> What would you like to do if you become a parent?
> What sometimes makes it hard for parents to do the right thing?

In closing, group members label and put away any drawings, name cards, etc. in their individual folders. Finally, the leader asks the children to share something they liked and did not like about the group session today, then reviews the name of the cameraperson for next week and reminds that child to come fifteen minutes early.

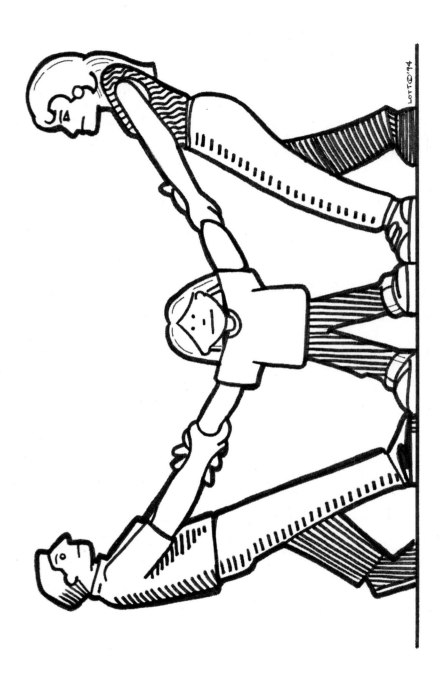

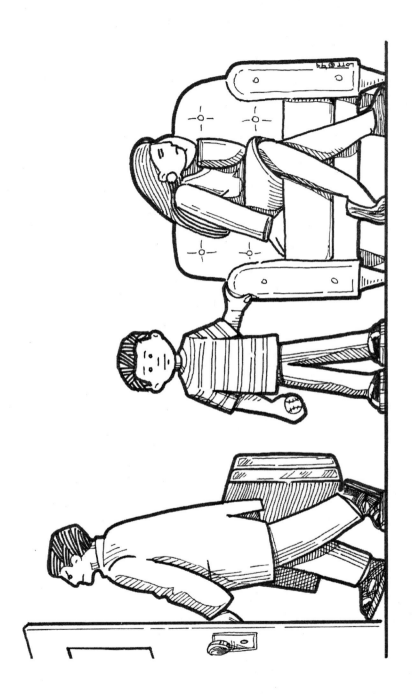

Exploring a Safe Inside Place
and Back to Reality

Goals

To help the children explore private hopes and wishes in a safe
inner place

To help the children identify feelings and thoughts when they go
back and forth between parents in the zone of conflict

Materials

Note: Materials starred with an asterisk (*) are reproduced in the
manual at the end of the session.

Video camera and monitor

Rules chart (posted in group room)

Feelings/color chart developed in Session 1 (posted in group
room)

Name tags and folders (to be kept in leader's possession)

Plenty of paper, pencils, markers, and rulers

Construction paper folded to look like a gift card, one piece for
each child (plus extras for mistakes)

*Picture of child going between two houses

Procedure

A. Warm-Up

When the group is seated in a circle or around a table, the leader
makes a brief statement of welcome. Then the group begins with

check-in, which involves asking each child to say something about her or his day and choose a feeling word to describe how she or he is feeling at that time. The children are encouraged to use words from the list created during the first session or to use one of their own, which can then be added to the list if the group or leader wishes. The leader then reminds the group who the cameraperson is for that day.

B. Relaxation

Clinical note: The focus of these relaxation exercises is on awareness and mastery of physical tension states. For younger or less mature groups, these introductory activities can be done without the guided visualization, using the "smell the cookies, blow out the candles" exercise described at the beginning of Session 3. Separate instructions are given for groups that are visualizing before drawing and for groups that are drawing only.

The leader says in his or her own words:

> Remember, in the last session you were learning to relax a little. Let's see how many of you have your shoulders attached to your earlobes right now. [Leader demonstrates with tense shoulders.] Let's try to get these shoulders relaxed. I will count down from ten to zero. You can close your eyes if you like.

C. The Gift

For groups that are visualizing, instructions begin here. For groups that are drawing only, go directly to C1 following.
The leader says in her or his own words:

> With your eyes still closed, I want you to imagine the door to your special private room. Can you see it? Open it and look around. Notice if the room you drew has changed at all. Is it the same? [Pause] Different? [Pause] Now imagine that a gift to you has appeared on the doorstep of your private room, which you drew last week. You walk over to it. Is it large? Small? Open your gift. It is special, exactly what you want. Enjoy it for a few minutes. [Pause] There is a card attached to your gift. Read it. [Pause] What does it say? Does it say who your gift is from?

[Pause] Now decide if you wish to leave it in the room or bring it out. [Pause] Now I will count back down from ten to zero. At ten you will begin to leave your room and slowly come back to the group, and arrive back here at zero.

The leader counts slowly back from ten to zero, then says in her or his own words:

Now, while we're still relaxed, I want you to take a few minutes to draw your gift into the picture of the room. You can draw on a separate sheet of paper and attach it to your room if you like. After you have done this, write down, in private, what the gift card says.

The leader distributes folded paper for the gift card message. The leader invites but does not press group members to share when they have finished the activity.

C1. The Gift

For groups that are drawing only, instructions begin here.
The leader says in his or her own words:

I want you to imagine that a gift to you has appeared in your private room, which you drew last week. The gift is really special, something that you really want. Try to decide what it is. Also, there is a card attached. Try to decide who the gift is from and what the card says. Now take a few minutes and draw your gift into the drawing of your room. You can draw on a separate sheet of paper and then attach it to your room if you like. Then write down what your gift card says. Attach that to your room also.

The leader distributes extra paper as needed for the gift drawing and folded paper for the gift card message. The leader invites but does not press group members to share when they have finished the activity.

D. Role-Play of Child Going Between Houses

The leader says in her or his own words:

Last time we talked about how it feels to be caught in the middle of our parents (or the grown-ups who care for us). Sometimes the feeling of being caught like that comes up when you go back and forth between your parents. Some of them live in separate houses, and some don't; either way it can be difficult going back and forth in an angry space between parents. Even when you love them both, you may have a lot of different feelings. Take a look at this picture. Can you think of a time when something happened that you didn't like, or maybe just didn't understand, when you were going between parents? Think of that time now. Who would like to direct a role-play about that?

Videotape the role-play. During the role-plays, the leader focuses on eliciting the feelings of the child toward the parents. When role-plays are done, the leader may ask in his or her own words:

Do parents sometimes act in ways that are difficult to understand? Would it help if parents explained what they were feeling and who they are upset with [if they are upset] and why? Is there another way that parents could handle their relationship and the space between them that would make it easier for the child?

If there is time, the leader helps the children to develop a role-play about an alternative way of going back and forth in the space between parents.

E. Video Review and Snack

The children are asked to sit around the table or in the original circle to get ready to end the group. The leader asks each child what he or she wants, then distributes the snack. During snack, the role-plays are reviewed on the monitor. The leader talks about the connections between feelings and behavior at transitions (e.g., "Sometimes when you come home to your mom, you kind of miss your dad and you feel sad or irritable" or, "Sometimes it feels like the divorce is happening all over again when you see your dad drive off" or, "When you hear your dad say unkind things about your mom, it sometimes kind of hurts inside"). The leader asks if anyone has figured out a way to feel better about going back and forth.

F. Closure and Housekeeping

Remember to be aware that the exercises during the session may have raised the children's anxiety. If so, the children are invited again to talk about ways they can keep themselves safe, and these ideas are added to the list. Each child is also asked to name one thing he or she liked and did not like about group today. Group members label and put away any drawings, name cards, and so on in their individual folders. A cameraperson is chosen for the next session.

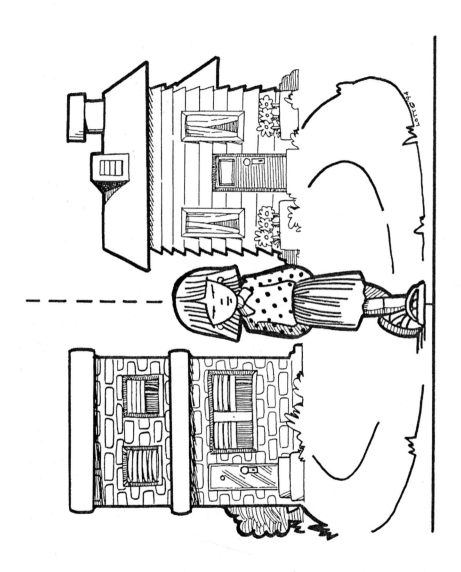

Defining Wishes for Yourself and Rules That Work for Your Family and Relationships

Goals

> To clarify roles and boundaries in families
> To help the children dramatize specific conflict situations so that their thoughts and feelings can be identified, fantasies and wishes can be clarified and reality tested, and issues of right and wrong can be discussed
> To help the children construct a code of ethics or rules for relationships

Materials

Note: Materials starred with an asterisk (*) are reproduced in the manual at the end of the session.

> Video camera and monitor
> Rules chart (posted in group room)
> Feelings/color chart developed in Session 1 (posted in group room)
> Name tags and folders (to be kept in leader's possession)
> Plenty of paper, pencils, markers, and rulers
> Envelopes and tape for groups who are not doing visualization during relaxation
> *Picture of child watching parents fight
> Flip chart and markers

Procedure

A. Warm-Up

When the group is seated in a circle or around a table, the leader makes a brief statement of welcome. Then the group begins with check-in, which involves asking each child to say something about her or his day and choose a feeling word to describe how she or he is feeling at that time. The children are encouraged to use words from the list or to use one of their own, which can then be added to the list if the group or leader wishes. If a child is having difficulty with the exercise, see the beginning of Session 2 for suggestions. The leader then reminds the group who the cameraperson is for that day.

B. Relaxation

To help the younger children relax, the leader may say:

> Sit up and put your hands on your tummies. Pretend you're smelling cookies (or pizza), and breathe in through your nose. Then, pretend you're blowing out candles (cooling the pizza), and blow the air out through your mouth. Ready? Okay, let's all practice.

For older children, the leader says in his or her own words:

> Let's check in and see how tense or relaxed we all are. Check your shoulders. Scrunch them up tight, then let them flop. Again. Now let's check arms. Make a fist and hold your arm out tightly in front of you. Now relax; let your arm get heavy and fall. Again. Okay. Now I will count down from ten to zero, so that you can spend a little time in your own space. You can close your eyes if you like.

C. The Private Wish

For groups that are visualizing, instructions begin here. For groups that are drawing only, go directly to C1 following.

The leader counts down slowly, then says in her or his own words:

> With your eyes still closed, I want you to imagine the door to
> your special private room. Can you see it? Is it the same?
> [Pause] Is it different? [Pause] Now go in and look around. Is it
> the same this week? [Pause] Any changes? [Pause] Now imag-
> ine that on one wall there is a very large blackboard that you
> have never noticed before. [Pause] Can you see it? [Pause]
> There is chalk and an eraser. You walk up to it. [Pause] Touch
> the board. [Pause] Pick up the chalk. [Pause] Now imagine that
> you are writing one thing you wish or think (maybe about some-
> one or something in your family) but never say out loud. [Long
> pause] It can be any wish at all that is yours and yours alone.
> I will not ask you to write it down or share it when we're done,
> unless you want to. [Pause again] Now decide if you wish
> to erase your message or leave it on the board. [Pause] Now I
> will count back up from zero to ten. At zero you will begin to
> leave your room and slowly come back to the group, and arrive
> at ten.

The leader then counts slowly from zero to ten.

Children are then asked to add a blackboard to their drawing of the
room and to write their private wishes on that blackboard, or they
may use a separate sheet of paper, insert it into an envelope, and attach it to their drawing of the room. The leader invites but does not
press for sharing and then moves on to the next activity.

C1. The Private Wish

For groups that are drawing only, instructions begin here.

The leader asks the children to add a blackboard to their rooms.
The leader then asks each child to write on a piece of paper three private wishes that they would write on their blackboard. The leader explains that these may be wishes that they have not told anyone, and
maybe have not felt safe telling anyone. The leader explains further
that, in order to keep the wishes private, they are to place them in an
envelope and then seal and tape the envelope at the end of the activity.
The leader invites but does not press for sharing and then moves on to
the next activity.

D. Jobs for People in Your Family

Clinical note: The emphasis here is on clarifying appropriate role boundaries and areas of responsibility within families.

The leader has the children sit around the table (in front of the flip chart) to generate a list of kids' jobs, rights, and responsibilities in a family and parents' jobs, rights, and responsibilities. The leader writes all suggestions on the chart, possibly clustering them into appropriate areas for later general classification (an example follows).

Jobs Chart

Parents/Adults	*Kids*
Outside-Home Jobs	*Outside-Home Jobs*
Go to work, earn money	Go to school, get good grades, be a good team member
Child Rearing/Caring for One Another Jobs	*At-Home Jobs*
Love and protect kids, discipline kids, stop fights	Do chores, obey parents, love parents, be nice to brother/sister
Inside-Home Jobs	*Self-Care Jobs*
Cook food, do household chores, yard work, washing, and so on	Relax and watch TV, play with friends
Self-Care Jobs	
Enjoy self, relax, see friends, party, date	

The leader also tries to have the children generate rules for the ways people should treat one another generally (especially peers, siblings, and parents): Be polite, kind, and gentle; don't hit, push, or shove; no put-downs; listen to others; keep an open mind; don't interrupt; take turns or share; and so on. (It is not necessary to push the children too far in generating this list, because during the role-plays that follow they will be adding new ones.)

E. Role-Plays About Right and Wrong

Clinical note: The focus is on developing and affirming codes of moral conduct in relationships.

The leader either presents the stimulus picture (child watching parents fight) or has the children recall and talk about an argument or fight someone had in their family and/or among their peers. (It is useful to ask for one example from home and one from school.) This can be a specific example or a composite script of what often happens. The leader helps the children to discuss the details and then has the group produce a role-play of the situation (using a director, camera-person, and actors as developed in previous sessions).

Clinical note: It may be useful to consider whether the children can realistically do anything about the fighting or whether it is simply better for the children to make a promise to themselves that they will live by different rules when they get older.

The leader can ask in his or her own words: "In the family that you would like to have, how would you like to treat your husband/wife/children? How would you like them to treat you?"

The leader discusses the details of the amended situation and, if appropriate, helps the children to develop a second role-play of that situation. The leader repeats the previous cycle, leaving about twenty minutes for section F1 or F2 following.

F1. Review of Rules and Snack (For Older Children)

Clinical note: The focus is to help the children to clarify and revise principles of moral conduct in relationships. This is also an opportunity to discuss safety planning when children bring up the problem of being in a dangerous situation.

While the older children are eating snack, the role-plays are reviewed on the monitor. It is the leader's task to frame the specific moral dilemma for the child in that situation: "What should the child do, and why?" The leader helps to tease out the different implications for each family member for the various solutions. Securing the child's safety in a dangerous situation is the top priority, and specific, practical measures need to be listed (for example, when to call 911 and whom to ask for help).

In addition, the product of this discussion is the elaboration of principles for what is fair, right, proper, unfair, wrong, and improper and under what conditions. These principles should be recorded on the flip chart and elaborated when further group discussions clarify them. Examples:

1. It is never okay for parents to hit each other.
2. It is okay to keep a secret from one's parent about the other parent if it is not his or her business.
3. It is not fair for kids to be asked to take sides.
4. It's okay for a kid to say that, if it feels safe. If not, it's okay just to think it.
5. Parents and their grown-up friends should be polite about one another in front of their children.

Finally, the leader has the children briefly discuss appropriate amends or restitution in each situation (e.g., apologies, promises not to repeat the offense, repair of the damage, fines, and promises to try harder in the future).

F2. Review of Jobs and Snack (For Younger Children)

Clinical note: The focus here is on concretely clarifying boundaries and identifying what is right and expected in family relationships. Many children from violent and dysfunctional families are burdened by inappropriate caretaking responsibilities. However, it is important to respect the fact that different cultures and ethnic groups have different expectations about parents' and children's roles or jobs within the family. The important distinction the leader needs to make is whether the roles or jobs that the children are taking on appear to be within their capabilities, or whether they are overburdening.

While the younger children are eating snack, the role-plays are reviewed on the monitor. The leader's questions should include the following:

What is the child trying to do here?
Is this a kid's job?
Is this a parent's job?

The leader checks the role-play against the chart and notices whether the child is doing his or her jobs. If the child is doing more than is expected, the leader notes this and affirms the moral or good intentions. The leader helps the children to decide whether doing extra is getting in the way of their doing their kids' jobs. The leader notes that the child/parent may be trying to do the right thing, but is going about it the wrong way and breaking the rules on how we should treat one another. The leader may ask, "Is it okay to scream, push, insult, ignore others' views, or hurt others' feelings?" From this discussion, new rules are generated and written on the chart. Finally, the leader briefly discusses appropriate amends or restitution in each situation (e.g., apologies, promises not to repeat the offense, and repair of damage).

Clinical note: When discussing role-plays of real-life situations, it is important not to further tarnish the child's view of a parent. It is important to note the following:

> Everyone is allowed to make mistakes. No one is perfect.
> Sometimes when people are angry, upset, or under a lot of stress, they do and say things that they shouldn't.

It is also important to save the child's "face" when it was determined that she or he had broken the rule/principle, by giving lots of credit and appreciation for honesty and good intentions or recognizing the child's lack of knowledge.

G. Closure and Housekeeping

It is important to be aware that the exercises during this session may have raised fearful memories or anxiety. If so, the children are invited again to talk about ways they can keep themselves safe, and these ideas are added to the list. Then, each child is asked to name one thing she or he liked and did not like today. The leader collects name tags and any artwork that the children produced. The leader makes sure that the work has the child's name on it and places it in the appropriate folder. The leader identifies the cameraperson for the next session.

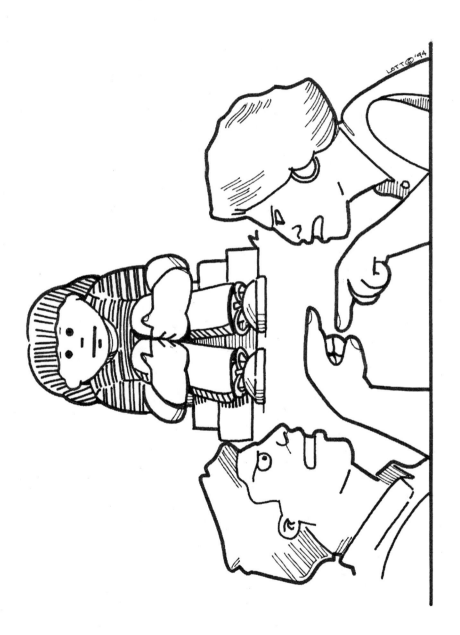

Exploring the Mirror: Who You Are and How You Show Your Feelings

Goals

To encourage self-definition and understanding in a safe inner space

To help the children understand the difference between feelings and action

To help explore nuance and complexity and tolerate ambiguity and ambivalence

Materials

Video camera and monitor

Rules chart (posted in group room)

Feelings/color chart developed in Session 1 (posted in group room)

Name tags and folders (to be kept in leader's possession)

Plenty of paper, pencils, markers, and rulers

Feelings measure charts developed in Session 2 (from each child's folder)

Procedure

A. Warm-Up

When the group is seated in a circle or around a table, the leader makes a brief statement of welcome. Then the group begins with check-in, which involves asking each child to say something about his or her day and choose a feeling word to describe how he or she is feeling at that time. The children are encouraged to use words from the list created during the earlier sessions or to use one of their own, which can then be added if the group or leader wishes. If a child is having difficulty with the exercise, see the beginning of Session 2 for suggestions. The leader then reminds the group who the camera-person is for that day.

B. Relaxation

The leader says in his or her own words:

> For younger children: "Okay, let's put our hands on our tummies and smell the cookies and blow out the candles. Repeat five times."
>
> For older children: "Okay, let's see where those shoulders are today. Try to hunch up to your ear lobes and then relax. Again."

The leader briefly encourages the group to note places of tension and to deliberately tighten up arms, legs, and so on, then let go. The leader then says in her or his own words: "Now, I'm going to count down from ten to zero. While I do so, I want you to relax, breathe in, and breathe out." The leader counts slowly from ten to zero, gently encouraging the group to relax and breathe deeply. When the group is relaxed, the leader proceeds to the mirror activity.

C. The Mirror

For groups that are visualizing, instructions are here. For groups that are drawing only, go directly to C1 following.

Clinical note: This exercise is designed to encourage the children to define and understand themselves more clearly and to think about who they want to be in the future.

The leader says in his or her own words, pausing at appropriate places:

> Now you are at the door to your private room. You go in. Has the room changed at all from last time? Is it the same? Take a little time to walk around in your mind and notice the things you decided to put in this private place. Notice how nice it is that no

one can come in and bother your things! Now, as you look around, you will see a mirror on one wall of your room. It may be new. Decide if your mirror is large or small. Does it show only your face or your whole body? Is the mirror fancy or plain? Now you can get fairly close to the mirror. Is it light or dark? Can you see well or not? Take a look in the mirror now. Is it difficult to look at yourself? How do you feel as you do this? Do you get tensed up? Try to relax. See what you like about yourself in that mirror. Is there anything you would like to change? What would you like to change now, or as you get older? Maybe you would just like to get a good look. Some kids have a difficult time seeing themselves clearly. Take time to do that now. Now, I'd like you to get ready to leave your mirror. Before you do, take a last look. Pay attention to what you saw that you liked. You may be surprised. Pay attention to anything you have promised to change. You might be surprised by that, too. Now, I'm going to count up from zero to ten. Stay relaxed as I do so, and then we can draw or write a little about our mirrors.

The leader counts gently and slowly from zero to ten and then distributes paper and markers. The leader invites the group to draw what they saw or to list what they liked and what they would like to change. After ten minutes or so (or when the group begins to lose focus), invite anyone who wishes to do so to share what she or he has drawn or written. Have children put their names on their work, collect it, and place it in the folders.

C1. The Mirror

For groups that are drawing only, instructions begin here.

Clinical note: This is a challenging exercise, and no child is forced to draw this picture. Some may be more comfortable writing a description in words. Those who refuse to do anything at all can be asked what they would have drawn, with the leader asking something such as "What do you like about what you see? What would you change if you could?"

The leader says in his or her own words:

I want you to imagine for a minute that you are looking in a mirror. Or, if you like, just remember the last time you saw yourself in the mirror. Try to think about what you like about yourself in that mirror. Is there anything you'd like to change? Anything you'd like to change now, or as you get older?

The leader then invites the group to draw what they saw or to list what they liked and what they would like to change. These productions can be attached to the pictures of internal rooms, collected, and placed in each child's folder.

D. How to Act on Feelings

Clinical note: The focus is on helping the children to understand that feelings need not always be expressed in action. It is in the domain of action that control is possible.

The leader distributes the feelings/measure charts from Session 2 and says in her or his own words: "You may remember that we talked about feelings in our second meeting, and I recall . . ."

It is important for the leader to recall, briefly, some information about each child's participation in that activity at that time. The children's sense of being heard, understood, and kept in mind is *very important*. The leader then says:

> Feelings are never wrong. People can't help what they feel. It's important to know how you feel and it's important to know how other people feel. However, there are right and wrong ways to *act* on your feelings. For instance, it's wrong to hit or beat up on people just because you're mad at them. There are wise and unwise ways to express your feelings. For example, telling your teacher she or he is stupid is probably not a good idea. Also, there are helpful and unhelpful ways to express your feelings. For instance, sometimes running away when you are scared helps and sometimes it doesn't. Telling a lie when you are afraid of getting into trouble does not help and usually gets you into even more trouble.

The leader then invites the group to identify one helpful or unhelpful way that they may have acted on a feeling that they listed on their feelings/measure charts from Session 2.

E. Role-Plays of Feelings and Actions

The leader asks the group to come up with situations (at home or at school) in which people had strong or big feelings and acted on them in a way that got them in trouble. The leader has the children role-play and videotape the situation, then asks them to do a second role-play, showing a better or more appropriate way of expressing those feelings in that situation. The group continues with role-playing in this manner until about fifteen minutes before the end of group.

F. Snack and Discussion

The children are asked to sit around the table or in the original circle to get ready for the end of group. The leader asks each child what she or he wants, then distributes the snack. While the children are eating snack, and after the video for the day has been reviewed, the leader finishes up the role-playing activity with a summation of five facts:

1. Feelings and behavior are different sometimes, so feelings are hard to figure out.
2. Sometimes people hide their feelings and act one way when they feel another.
3. Sometimes people freeze up like rocks when they are afraid of their feelings.
4. There are right and wrong ways to act on your feelings.
5. There might be safe ways to show your feelings, either to a safe person or just to yourself in your own private space.

G. Closure and Housekeeping

It is important to be aware that the exercises during the session may have raised fearful memories or anxiety. If so, the children are invited again to talk about ways they can keep themselves safe, and these ideas added to the list. Each child is then asked what he or she did and did not like about group today. Then, the leader collects and labels all work from the session and places it in the children's folders, collects name tags, and designates a cameraperson for the next session.

Exploring Your Inside Self and Your Outside Self

Goals

To help the children define and understand the difference between an inside self and an outside self

To help the children understand that feelings get masked but are still there

To help the children become aware that it is possible to decide why, when, and how to mask feelings

Materials

Note: All materials starred with an asterisk (*) are reproduced in the manual at the end of the session.

Video camera and monitor

Rules chart (posted in group room)

Feelings/color chart developed in Session 1 (posted in group room)

Name tags and folders (to be kept in leader's possession)

Plenty of paper, pencils, markers, and rulers

*Blank figure: Two pieces of paper stapled back to back, each with an identical blank figure; one set for each group member plus extras for mistakes or revisions

Blank white paper plates

*Sheet of faces with different expressions (enlarge photocopies of figures and faces provided on pages 154 and 155)

Procedure

A. Warm-Up

When the group is seated in a circle or around a table, the leader makes a brief statement of welcome. Then the group begins with check-in, which involves asking each child to say something about his or her day and choose a feeling word to describe how he or she is feeling at that time. The children are encouraged to use words from the list created during Session 1, or to use one of their own, which can then be added to the list if the group or leader wishes. If a child is having difficulty with the exercise, see the beginning of Session 2 for suggestions. The leader then reminds the group who the cameraperson is for that day.

B. Relaxation

Using either the "smell the cookies, blow out the candles "exercise" or the "count down from ten to zero" exercise, the leader briefly encourages the group to note places of tension and to deliberately tighten up arms, legs, and so on, then let go. The leader says in her or his own words:

> Now, I'm going to count down from ten to zero. While I do so, I want you to relax, breathe in, and breathe out.

The leader counts slowly from ten to zero, gently encouraging the group to relax and breathe deeply. When the leader determines that all the children are sufficiently relaxed, she or he proceeds to the statue activity.

C. The Statue

Clinical note: This activity is designed to encourage children to think about whether and how they show their inner selves to others.

For groups that are visualizing, the instructions begin here. For groups that are drawing only, go directly to C1 following. The leader says in her or his own words, pausing at appropriate places:

Now you are at the door to your private room. Notice how well you are getting to know your own special place. Has the room changed at all from last time? Is it the same? Now, as you look around, you will see, in a kind of dark corner, a statue or sculpture of yourself as you really are. Slowly the light becomes brighter, and you can discover more about the statue. Is it small or tall? What shape is it in? What is the statue doing? Walk all around the statue and look at it. Now, I want you to imagine that you have become this statue. Imagine that you are this statue. What do you do? Now, become yourself again and look at this statue. Does the statue seem any different to you now? Has anything changed? Slowly, get ready to say good-bye to the statue and come back to the group as I count to ten. Say good-bye to your statue now.

The leader counts slowly from zero to ten and then invites each group member to become their statue again, for the group, and tell briefly what it is like to be a statue and what the statue does when it comes to life.

C1. The Statue

For groups that are drawing, instructions begin here.

The leader says in his or her own words: "I want you to imagine for a minute that you are a statue. Try to imagine what kind of statue you would be. What shape? What size? What is the statue doing? Now draw that statue."

The leader then invites each group member to become their statue and tell briefly what it is like to be a statue and what the statue does when it comes to life.

D. Inside Me/Outside Me

Clinical note: The focus of this activity is on helping the children to define and understand the difference between an inside self and an outside self.

The leader says in his or her own words: "We're going to be talking a bit more today about how we show feelings. Let's just do a little exercise to get started."

The leader holds up the sheet showing faces with different expressions (see Materials section) and asks the group to try to identify the feeling each face expresses.

Clinical note: It is important to emphasize that not everyone may agree about what the feeling is and that it is not always possible to tell, from the outside, what the inside feelings are.

The leader then says in her or his own words:

> Today we are going to think a bit about how we all keep some of our feelings inside, how what we show other people and what we really feel inside are sometimes different. Usually we do that to feel safe or because we think our feelings are not okay. Everyone does it. Right now, I want you to remember something that happened in your own family that made you feel like hiding your feelings. You don't have to share it right now. I want you to think about yourself in that memory. Maybe you are remembering a family meeting, or the day your parents told you they were getting divorced, or the day someone came to visit. Whatever. Think about yourself in that memory. Where were you? What were you wearing? What were you doing? Were you inside or outside? Was the day warm or cold? Remember whatever you can. When you have done that, think about how you felt. Look at the feelings on our feelings/color chart. Which one fit for you then?
>
> Did you have a lot of feeling? Did you have mixed feelings? Did you feel more than one thing?
>
> Now, I want you to take the two stapled pieces of paper with blank figures on them and use our feelings/color chart to fill in these feelings from your memory on the figure on the bottom side of the paper. These are your inside feelings.
>
> When you have done the inside feelings, think about how you acted at the time of your memory. Were you quiet? Were you noisy? Did you cry or look sad? Did you go away and think about something else? Did you get angry or smile? Think about whether you let your inside feelings show. Now, take your outside figure, the one on the top sheet, and fill it in, showing us

your outside feelings. Sometimes they're the same as inside feelings, sometimes they're not.

Clinical note: Younger children may produce the same feelings on the inside and on the outside. Older children who are anxious may do the same. What is valuable is introducing the idea that the inside and the outside may be different.

When the task is complete, the children are invited to share their productions.

E. Masks and Role-Plays

Clinical note: The focus is on helping the children to be aware of what they present to others and what they mask, as well as to consider when, where, and with whom it is safe to remove the mask and be real.

Masks. The leader distributes paper, pens, and paper plates to each child. The leader says in his or her own words: "Sometimes we put on a face (like one of those we saw earlier), to hide our real feelings inside. Let's call this 'using a mask.'"

The leader asks the children to give the reasons why we sometimes hide our real feelings or use a mask (e.g., to avoid hurting other people's feelings, to stop someone from being angry at you, to get someone to give you something you want, to please other people, to keep your own real feelings private, and so on). The leader may suggest more concrete ideas such as the following:

> Grandmother comes to visit and brings awful cookies.
> You just stepped in something stinky, but you don't want your friends to know.
> Your puppy just chewed up the rug. You just found it, and now your mom or dad walks in!

It is important for the leader to emphasize that masks are valuable. The leader is not to challenge the mask in any way; rather, the leader is to help the children become aware of their masks so that they can be used effectively.

The leader then asks the children to think of a situation (at home or at school) where they used a mask. The leader asks the group to think about what their real feelings were underneath and the kind of face or outside feelings they showed to others, then instructs the children to make masks of their outside faces using colored pens and paper plates. After this is completed, the children may show one another the masks they have made and explain a bit about the situation in which they remembered using them. The leader asks the children to identify some of their real feelings underneath (using the feelings/color chart as a prompt). Some children prefer to put their inside feelings on the back of their masks and flip it over during the role-play to reveal their true feelings.

Role-plays. The leader invites volunteers or encourages the children to take turns role-playing the real-life situation, using the masks. The instructions are for the child to play herself or himself holding the mask in front of her or his face. Every so often during the role-play, the child removes the mask (which is a signal for the other role-players to freeze), looks directly at the camera, and says how she or he really feels. Then the mask is replaced and the role-play continues.

F. Snack and Video Review of Role-Plays

The children are asked to sit around the table or in the original circle to get ready for the end of group. The leader asks each child what he or she wants, then distributes the snack. During the snack, the video segments of the role-plays are reviewed and discussed. The leader encourages the children to talk about why the masks were needed. Reasons may include the following: to keep from hurting another's feelings, to get someone's cooperation, to keep something private, and so on. In addition, the leader may ask the group to generate a list of situations in which the use of a mask is questionable (e.g., to lie or to get something you want at the expense of another). Also, the leader may comment that if you hide your true feelings all the time, people don't really know you, you can be very lonely, and other people can't give you what you really want; or you might get into a habit of pleasing others all the time and never please yourself; and so on.

G. Closure and Housekeeping

As usual, it is important to be aware that the exercises during the session may have raised fearful memories or anxiety. If so, the children are invited to talk about ways they can keep themselves safe.

Then the children are asked to name one thing they did or did not lik about group today, before the leader collects and labels all work from the session and places it in the children's folders, collects name tags, and designates a cameraperson for the next session.

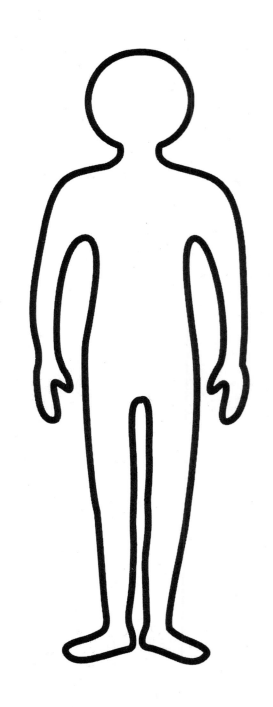

Making a Family Sculpture:
Who We Are and Who We Could Be

Goals

To help restore or build a capacity for healthy idealism and hope for one's future

To help the children to be more conscious of choices about who they are and will become

To help the children consider using their safe inner place in situations outside of group

To help the children begin to anticipate the end of group

To help the children become aware (and more in control) of their positions in their families and their rules and expectations about relationships

Materials

Note: Materials starred with an asterisk (*) are reproduced in the manual at the end of the session.

Video camera and monitor

Rules chart (posted in group room)

Feelings/color chart developed in Session 1 (posted in group room)

Name tags and folders (to be kept in leader's possession)

Plenty of paper, pencils, markers, and rulers

Small paper cups (two for each group member)

*Two apple seed cutout shapes for each child (one to use, one extra), large enough to have two or three sentences printed on them

Procedure

A. Warm-Up

When the group is seated in a circle or around a table, the leader says a brief word of welcome and acknowledges each child individually while distributing name tags and noting who the cameraperson is for the day. Then the group begins with check-in, which involves asking each child to say something about his or her day and choose a feeling word to describe how he or she is feeling at that time. The children are encouraged to use words from the list created during earlier sessions or to use one of their own, which can then be added to the list if the group or leader wishes.

B. Relaxation

Then the leader says in his or her own words:

> After today, we will have two more meetings together and then we'll go our separate ways for a few months. After that, we'll get to meet together once more, just to check in and say hello and see how we're all doing. Today we're going to spend some time thinking about how you can use your private room when you aren't in group, like when you're at home, at school, or alone. First, let's try to relax.

Using the "smell the cookies, blow out the candles" or the "count down from ten to zero" exercise, the leader briefly encourages the group to note places of tension and to deliberately tighten up arms, legs, and so on, and then let go. After a few moments, when the leader feels that the group is relaxed and focused, they can proceed to the keys to the room activity.

C1. Keys to the Room

For groups that are visualizing only.

Clinical note: This exercise is designed to help the children understand that they can access a private inner space both in and outside of group. It is also designed to help the children begin to think about who they are becoming and how they may influence that process and outcome. Again, safety planning may need to be discussed during this exercise. The children need to know when it is safe to enter into a private fantasy space for protection and when they need to take practical steps to remove themselves from a dangerous situation.

The leader says in his or her own words: "Now you are going to visit your private room. I'm going to count down from ten to zero. While I do so, I want you to relax, breathe in, and breathe out." The leader counts slowly from ten to zero, gently encouraging the group to relax and breathe deeply. The leader then says in her or his own words, pausing at appropriate places:

> Now you are at the door to your private room. Notice the size and shape of the door. Notice the color of the door. Now you are ready to enter this place that has become your own. Has the room changed at all from last time? I want you to give yourself a chance to think about this room that you have made for yourself at the age you are now. Notice the colors, the mirror—remember the mirror? The gift? The blackboard? You may wish to come into this room even when you are not meeting with the group, at times when you are at home or in school or alone and you just need a safe place to be with yourself. Look around you—this room will always be here for you, now and even as you get older. It is a safe and protected place. Now let's get ready to leave our rooms, but just for a moment, because we'll be coming back a couple of times. We'll practice getting in and out of this room whenever we need to. I'll count slowly from zero to ten. While I do so, you will leave your room, gently close the door, and then come back to us in the group.

The leader counts from zero to ten, intermittently instructing the group to slowly leave, close the door, and so on, then says:

> Now let's practice getting to our own safe places when we want to. I will start you off, and then you will do a couple of trips to your room alone. Notice how you get yourself into your room space.

The leader could then discuss the best times to enter their private space:

Sometimes it is good for you to go into your private space—when you don't want to be bothered by anyone—when you want to be quiet, alone, and separate. Other times, it might not be such a good idea to go off to your private space. For example, if your big brother is punching your little sister really hard, it might be best to go and get a grown-up to help out! What other times might it be best to make sure that you or someone else is safe?

C2. A Wish for Tomorrow

For groups that are visualizing, the instructions begin here. For groups that are drawing only, proceed directly to C3 following.

Clinical note: The purpose of this exercise is to give children permission to dream about a better future and hope for things to be different and better when they are grown-ups than what they have experienced in the past. It is difficult for children who have experienced trauma to envision any kind of future, let alone one that is safe and pleasurable. This activity is a way for them to begin to imagine and conceptualize lives that do not follow the same paths as their families'.

The leader counts down slowly from ten to zero and guides the children back to their private rooms, then says in his or her own words:

Okay, now you're back in your room. I want you to think about who you will be when you become a grown-up. What will you be doing? How will that person be the same as you are now? How will that person be different from who you are now? Now I want you to make a promise to that grown-up you. It can be a promise about anything that has to do with helping you become what you want to be when you grow up. It is a private promise, and it is safe because you are making it in your private room. Now I want you to imagine that you are placing that promise to yourself in a seed that you will plant in your room. That seed will grow as you grow. Now imagine that you are planting your seed with the promise inside it, and you are placing it in a safe place in your room. Now I will count back up from zero to ten. While I do so, you will slowly leave your room again and rejoin the group.

When finished counting, the leader asks the children to write their promises on the paper seed provided, fold it, and drop it into their paper cups.

C3. A Wish for Tomorrow

For groups that are drawing only, the instructions begin here.
The leader says in her or his own words:

> Now I want you to think about who you will be when you are grown up. What will you be doing? How will that person be the same as you are now? How will that person be different? Now I want you to make a promise to yourself. It can be a promise about anything that has to do with helping you become who you want to be when you are an adult. It is a private promise. Now I want you to write that promise on this paper apple seed and then plant it in your Dixie cup. As you plant it, imagine that this promise will grow with you. You may wish to draw the growing seed on the picture of your room.

D1. Family Sculpture (Older Children)

Clinical note: The goal of the exercise is to help the children to be conscious of their roles in their families as well as their rules and expectations about relationships. This perspective can help the children to revise their rules and expectations in a more realistic way. If a child will not draw this, he or she can be encouraged to do a verbal description or narrative of what it is like for him or her at home.

The leader asks the group to explain what a sculpture is (e.g., a piece of art that shows feelings and ideas in a form that you can see and touch). The leader explains that "In this session we are going to use our bodies to create a sculpture to explain our feelings and ideas."

Practice. Split the children into small groups of three or four (it might be useful to divide the boys from the girls) to practice making sculptures using their body positions and facial expressions to represent the following contradictory feelings and ideas:

1. Feeling in charge, as if you can do what you want, versus feeling helpless, as if you have to do what another person wants

2. Feeling close versus feeling far apart
3. Hoping, praying that the other person will do what you want versus giving up and ignoring the other person or pretending you don't care
4. Feeling as if you belong and keeping someone close to you versus feeling as if you don't belong and feeling left out
5. Feeling embarrassed versus feeling proud
6. Fighting and arguing versus agreeing and cooperating
7. Doing something wrong and feeling bad versus punishing someone else and feeling mad

The small groups take turns representing, in still-life form, each of these scenes and guessing what is being represented. Next the leader has the group members sit around the table with paper and pens and asks them to map out sculptures of their families.

Children can elect to do a part of or the whole family situation, and some might choose to do two sculptures (one with Dad and one with Mom). The children may or may not play their own part in the family sculpture. The leader encourages expression of feelings about closeness/distance, inclusion/exclusion, conflict/cooperation, and so on in these scenarios. The children then take turns in setting up the family sculptures, which are then videotaped from all angles (one to two minutes for each).

D2. Family Sculpture (Younger Children)

The leader says in her or his own words:

> Today we're going to do some work being statues. We're going to make groups of statues that show opposite feelings. Let's talk about opposites for a minute. What is the opposite of up? Tall? Happy? Okay. Now we're going to try to show how opposite feelings, such as happy and sad, might look if they were statues.

The small groups take turns representing, as group statues, each of these scenes, holding them for thirty seconds or more. Next, the leader has the group members sit around the table with paper and pens and draw how they usually are with their families.

The leader asks in her or his own words: "What would each member look like if they were part of this group statue?"

Clinical note: If children are struggling with this exercise, the leader may modify the instructions for some or all group members, to draw how they usually are with one of their parents. Other children might choose to do two sculptures—one with Dad and one with Mom. If the child will not draw, he or she can be encouraged to give a verbal description or narrative of what it is like to be at home.

The children may or may not play their own part in the family sculpture. The leader encourages them to express their feelings about being close or far apart, being left out or belonging, fighting or getting along, and so on. The children then take turns setting up each group statue, which is then videotaped from all angles (take one to two minutes for each).

E. Fantasy Family Sculpture

When the videotaping of each sculpture or group statue is completed, the leader starts with the first sculpture and asks the child who set it up: "How would you change this to make it just the way you wish your family could be?" The leader can prompt, saying that this may involve ejecting certain members, bringing others in, or rearranging them in some way. The changed grouping is then videotaped from all angles.

Additional clinical notes: The ultimate goal is to help the children identify their particular rules and expectations about relationships (e.g., "in your family you have decided: don't have feelings, don't make demands; always be in control; be the central pivot that stops the family from falling apart; don't get too close to anyone; I am no good" etc.). Be warmly supportive and careful with any interpretation, emphasizing that this is an understandable way to feel and act: "You are just trying to survive; trying not to hurt your dad's feelings; trying not to get your mom angry at you; trying to take care of your mom; trying to be different from your brother; and so on."

Caution: These family sculptures can arouse powerful feelings in the children which, if not properly supported and worked through, can lead to anxiety and distress, acting out, or phobic avoidance when the child goes home or in future sessions. It is often helpful to predict that upsetting feelings may occur and invite the children to talk about them in a separate individual session.

F. Letter to Parents

Clinical note: This activity is designed to affirm the child's sense of self and boundaries. Although they will offer, the children are not allowed to do the writing on this activity. This is another opportunity for the leader to take the role of the adult and be in charge. By writing the list a child is trying to be in control, please the adult, and/or get distance from an anxiety-producing situation. The children may be anxious about if and when this letter will be given to their parents or guardians (usually this is done during parent group meetings). They may need reassurance that their individual contributions will not be identified.

The leader takes poster board or paper and pen and writes on the top: "Dear parents or family:" The leader then says in his or her own words:

> Now that we've thought about what it's like to be in our families, let's write a letter to them. We will list all the things we want them to know about how kids think and feel. Adults don't always understand what it's like for kids when there is fighting, when things change, when people leave and new people join the family, or many of the other things you have experienced. This is a great way to teach them about what it's like for all of you.

The leader facilitates and serves as scribe. When the letter is complete, all the children should come up and sign it.

G. Snack and Review

The children are asked to sit around the table or in the original circle to get ready for the end of group. The leader asks each child what she or he wants, then distributes the snack. During snack time, the children review their family sculptures on the video monitor. As each family scene is reviewed, the leader asks each child to talk about what feelings and ideas the sculpture represents and how each of the members is feeling, with special focus on the child. Questions to help the child process this experience might include the following points:

1. "What would you like to do in this situation?"
2. "If you weren't in this family, how would it be different?"
3. "If you spend a lot of time with your friends, will anything be different at home? Will your family be there for you when you get back?"
4. For children who have produced two entirely different, uncoordinated scenes in Mom's and Dad's houses, ask them to imagine one parent's household as audience to the other scene and vice versa: "Is this okay, to allow both Mom and Dad to watch what you are doing at the other parent's house?"

H. Closure and Housekeeping

Again, it is important to be aware that these exercises may have raised fearful memories or anxiety. The children are invited to talk about ways they can keep themselves safe, and these ideas added to the list. The children are each asked to name one thing they liked and one thing they did not like about group today. Then the leader collects name tags and any artwork the children have produced. The leader makes sure that the work has the children's names on it and places the work in the appropriate folder. The leader identifies the cameraperson for the next session and reminds the group that there will be two more sessions after today.

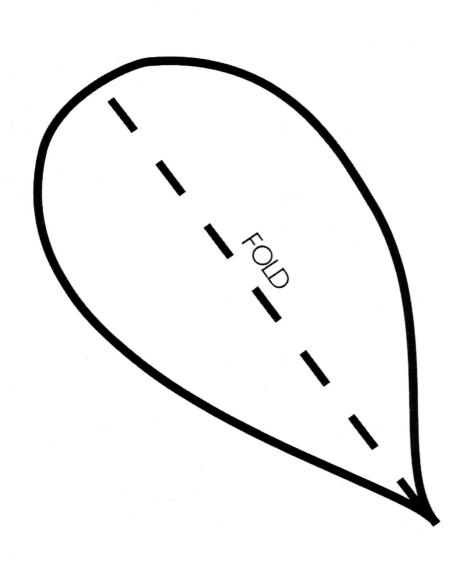
FOLD

Becoming the Experts on Living with Change, Loss, and Conflict

Goals

To encourage the children to see their peers as potential resources and sources of support

To encourage the children to share different ways of coping with dilemmas that are common in conflicted families

To help the children make moral decisions about how to resolve these dilemmas

Materials

Note: Materials starred with an asterisk (*) are reproduced in the manual at the end of the session.

Video camera and monitor

Rules chart (posted in group room)

Feelings/color chart developed in Session 1 (posted in group room)

Name tags and folders (to be kept in leader's possession)

Plenty of paper, pencils, markers, and rulers

Two or three balloons, straws, tape, glue, fabric scraps, Dixie cups, dry macaroni, and other materials appropriate for a small group sculpture

*Panel-of-experts questions/sample letters from other kids (These are developed by the leader for older groups and should reflect specific issues that members have shown, during group sessions, that they are struggling with.)

*Dilemma-situations pictures (provide enlarged photocopies)

Family jobs and general/rules charts generated during Session 5

Procedure

A. Warm-Up

When the group is seated in a circle or around a table, the leader says a brief word of welcome to the group and acknowledges each child individually while distributing name tags and noting the camera-person for the day. Then the group begins with check-in, which involves asking each child to say something about her or his day and choose a feeling word to describe how she or he is feeling at that time. The children are encouraged to use words from the list or to use one of their own, which can then be added to the list if the group or leader wishes.

B. Relaxation

Using the "smell the cookies, blow out the candles" or the "count down from ten to zero" exercise, the leader briefly encourages the group to note places of tension and to deliberately tighten up arms, legs, and so on, and then let go. The children can be given the opportunity to visit their private rooms, taking their time to enter, look around, and leave again.

C. Group Art Project

Clinical note: The focus of this activity is to have the children experience mastery through cooperation with their peers.

The leader says in his or her own words:

Today we're going to spend some time helping one another. You might find that other kids can be a big help sometimes, when you're stuck or when you just want to have some fun. Other kids, who are outside your family, can be really important in your life and can sometimes help you get over bad times when the family feels shaky. We'll start with a helping project.

The leader distributes materials for the group art project equally (see item 6 in Materials section) and explains that the group will have ten minutes in which to build a statue of a person, plus any other figure or things, in such a way that all the materials are included in the statue and added to the statue by the person who has possession of them. The rules are that the group may not speak, although they may communicate nonverbally (leader may need to demonstrate), and the group members may trade materials with other group members at any point if both agree. The leader begins timing when the project has been clearly explained. When the project is finished, the leader should comment positively on the statue and on the group members' ability to help one another make something so creative, unusual, etc. The leader should ask the group's permission to keep the statue to show other children their age who might not know, as well as this group does, how to work well with other children to get things done.

D1. TV Panel of Experts (For Older Children)

Clinical note: The focus of this activity is to consolidate new ideas about relationships and to encourage children to see their peers as a resource.

The leader says in her or his own words:

> Because you all have parents who sometimes/often have problems with cooperating, you have become something of an expert on how kids feel about difficult things in their families, especially parents' fighting. You also have a lot of good ideas on how kids can cope with the problems that come up. We are going to make a TV show in which you will be the panel of experts, like on _____ [Give examples of TV shows]. You are going to answer questions asked by other kids whose parents fight or are having other problems.

To heighten the seriousness of this task, the leader can also explain that not only parents but also other adults, such as judges, attorneys, mediators, counselors, and teachers, often really do not understand how children think and feel when parents fight or split up and that the children's answers will be an important way of teaching these adults. The leader explains that if the children give their written permission, he or she would like to use some of their words (but not their names) when talking to these adults, as well as to other children.

Practice. The leader reads the first one or two questions or letters (from examples in the list at the end of the session) and has the children practice their responses. The group then decides on a name for the TV program (e.g., *The Wide World of Divorce* or *The Wide World of Families*) and assigns a cameraperson and a talk-show host to take turns throughout the session. Then the talk-show host asks two or three questions (per segment), generating lots of discussion and alternative coping strategies among the group.

Each segment of the show is punctuated by short commercial breaks that the children make up. After each commercial, the talk-show host and cameraperson are rotated.

D2. Solving Dilemmas (For Younger Children)

The prompts for discussion and role-plays consist of the series of pictures that are included in the manual at the end of this session. The leader should select one of these pictures at a time (or substitute a new one, according to what would be appropriate and useful for the children in any particular group).

Discussion. The leader says in her or his own words:

> Take a look at this picture. What is happening here? What do you think the child is feeling? What do you think each adult is feeling? Did anything like this ever happen to you or anyone you know?

The leader then asks in her or his own words: "What do you think the child should do here?"

The leader generates many alternative coping responses, talks about different outcomes for these coping responses (i.e., evaluating the alternatives), and helps the group to decide on one of the better solutions. Again, safety planning in dangerous situations may be discussed.

Role-play. Have the children role-play the dilemma and the solution. Videotape this production. Ask if they feel okay about the solution and if not, why not?

Repeat this process with as many of the different dilemmas portrayed as time permits. (The leader can alternate between simply discussing the picture and deciding on solutions and actually role-playing, depending on the interest of the group.)

E. Snack and Video Review

Clinical notes: The focus of this activity is to clarify and affirm the rules of moral conduct in relationships.

The children are asked to sit around the table or in the original circle to get ready for the end of group. The leader asks each child what he or she wants, then distributes the snack. During snack, the video segments of the panel of experts are reviewed. This task naturally raises many moral dilemmas, which the children are prompted to address in further discussion. For older groups, the leader notes how the children's responses accord with the rules of moral conduct that they have generated in previous sessions.

For younger groups, it is important to validate different kinds of coping responses in different situations (e.g., assertive efforts, strategic withdrawal and avoidance, or seeking the help of others). It is also important for children to differentiate between what they can and cannot solve.

F. Closure and Housekeeping

In closing, the children are asked to state one thing they liked and one thing they did not like about group today. The leader collects name tags and any artwork the children have produced, makes sure that the work has the children's names on it, and places the work in the appropriate folder. The leader identifies the cameraperson for the next session and reminds the group that there will be one more session after today

Panel-of-Experts Questions

1. My parents cannot agree about how much time I spend with each of them. Sometimes I feel like I have to decide, but that's really difficult. What could I do?
2. Sometimes I feel like my mom loves me too much, like she won't let me out of her sight or something. I love my mom, but I love my dad and having my own life too. What should I do?
3. I wish my mother would spend more time with me than she does. How can I let her know how much she is hurting my feelings?

4. My dad drinks a lot of beer every night and gets drunk. What can I do to stop him?
5. My parents fight all the time. I feel like I have to take sides because if I don't they might not want me around. What do you think I should do?
6. My big brother got in trouble with the police and now he's in jail. Sometimes I wonder if that will happen to me.
7. My babysitter always wants to put his arms around me when we are watching TV. I feel uncomfortable about that. What can I do?
8. My parents act like they're totally in charge of the visitation schedule and I don't get to say what I want. Sometimes I want to just hang out or just get some attention on my own, for myself. What should I do?
9. My parents are fighting a lot and my dad hits my mom and my brother sometimes. I get really scared and worried about it. What can I do to stop them?
10. My stepdad thinks he's supposed to be in charge of me, but he's not. I don't like him. What can I do?
11. After my parents got a divorce and I saw how my dad treated my mom, I decided all men are creeps. What if I can never find a man to marry who is not a creep? What can you tell me about that?
12. My mother blames my dad for everything that goes wrong, and I wish that she would stop. What can I do about this?
13. My parents play favorites with us kids. When I'm the favorite, I feel sort of happy, but sad and mad that my brother is not the favorite and that he's mad at me about it. What can I do about this?
14. Sometimes I think that neither of my parents really wants me around. Do you have any ideas about that?

These questions should be modified and constructed to reflect those that are relevant to the children within the particular group.

Telling Your Story So Far, Thinking About Who You Want to Be in the Future, and Saying Good-Bye

Goals

To suggest that there can be a coherent story in many family conflicts, and the child can construct a coherent narrative for himself or herself

To help the older children consciously identify with or distance themselves from different aspects of both their parents

To help the younger children consider how to love and remain attached to both of their parents

To suggest coping strategies in a path to a better future

To achieve a sense of closure in the group and to say good-bye

Materials

Note: Materials starred with an asterisk (*) are reproduced in the manual at the end of the session.

Video camera and monitor

Rules chart (posted in group room)

Feelings/color chart developed in Session 1 (posted in group room)

Name tags and folders (to be kept in leader's possession)

Plenty of paper, pencils, markers, and rulers

*"The Turtle Story"

*Identity Shields (for older, school-age groups only). You will need sheets of white cardboard (11" x 8") for each child with

an outline for a coat of arms drawn on each sheet, colored
pens, pencils, scissors, and glue
*An award certificate for each child
Party food

Procedure

A. Warm-Up

When the group is seated in a circle or around a table, the leader
says a brief word of welcome to the group and acknowledges each
child individually while distributing name tags and noting the cameraperson for the day (for the younger groups of children only). Then the
group begins with check-in, which involves asking each child to say
something about his or her day and choose a feeling word to describe
how he or she is feeling at that time. The children are encouraged to
use words from the list or to use one of their own, which can then be
added to the list if the group or leader wishes.

B. Relaxation

Using the "smell the cookies, blow out the candles" or the "count
down from ten to zero" exercise, the leader briefly encourages the
group to note places of tension and to deliberately tighten up arms,
legs, and so on and then let go.

C. Story of the Divorce ("The Turtle Story")

Clinical note: The purpose of this exercise is to reduce confusion and
anxiety by providing children with a way to organize their understanding of parental conflict without blaming or taking sides. The
leader may decide to reword the story to reflect the concerns of children in families that are in conflict but do not divorce. See alternative
ending 2, for example.

Children are asked to make themselves comfortable (lean back and
close eyes). If possible, they can lie on a rug on the floor. The leader
says in her or his own words:

Now we are going to visit our private rooms once again. Try to relax your shoulders, your whole body. [Leader encourages the children to relax further by deliberately tensing and relaxing their muscles.] Now count yourself down from ten to zero. [Pause for about thirty seconds] [Add the following only for groups who are visualizing: "Notice now that you are at your door and can enter your special room whenever you're ready. Notice how your room is always there for you. Is it warm or cold? Get comfortable in your room."] Now I will tell you a story.

The leader narrates (or reads) "The Turtle Story" (see the end of the session). The leader asks the children whether they know why their parents got married/got together in the first place (what attracted them to each other), what changed over time, and what made them start to fight or separate.

Clinical note: Some children will be able to explain this better than others. Some may not be very interested. Do not push it with those who cannot or do not want to explain this. Invite those who are confused but interested to talk about it further with parents or the group leader in individual sessions, if possible.

D1. Identity Shields (For Older Children)

Clinical note: The purpose of this exercise is to introduce the idea that identifications can be consciously selected. The idea is to create a shield that shows what each child is striving for, an ideal that sets a standard rather than an expectation of unrealistic perfection.

The leader distributes the cardboard coat of arms to each child and says in his or her own words:

Each of you is beginning your own life's journey—going on a big adventure. You'll soon be teenagers and growing up. You want to be prepared for this special journey, a mission into the future, by taking things with you from your past. This includes different things from each of your parents (such as being a land turtle and a sea turtle), from other special people you have known or would like to know, as well as pieces that are uniquely you. You may also want to deliberately leave behind things that are not useful—from each of your parents and from these other people. There may also be parts of yourself you want to leave behind.

What you have in front of you is a shield for a coat of arms that will represent what you want to take with you in your journey into life. Notice that your coat of arms is divided into five parts. The top left corner represents your mom, the top right corner represents your dad, the two middle sections are for any two people who have been important to you in your life, and the bottom piece is you.

Using words or pictures, write or draw what you want to take with you from each person. On the blank area outside the shield, write or draw what you want to leave behind.

The children can keep their coats of arms private if they wish, or they might like to share them with the other group members at the end. When they have finished drawing, they are instructed to take the scissors and cut out the coat of arms, leaving the remainder behind.

Note: It is important to collect all the pieces later (including the discarded parts) so that the group leader can reconstruct and assess what each child did.

D2. "Turtle Story" Role-Play (For Younger Children)

Clinical note: This activity is designed to help younger children apply the ideas that are introduced in "The Turtle Story" to their understanding of their own family.

The leader invites the children to reenact "The Turtle Story" from beginning to end, acting out all the feelings that each of the turtle family members had, especially Tommy and Tina.

If time permits, this role-play can be repeated with different children playing the role of the young turtles. The children are invited to elaborate on the story in any way they wish. Their productions are videotaped. If there is time at the end of this activity (thirty minutes should be set aside for the closing sections of this session), the children can watch the videotapes and talk about the different feelings the young turtles had and how they expressed these feelings in the different role-plays.

Another option is to have the children illustrate the story, either at the end or as it is read. The group leader can initiate a discussion about who is like a "wise owl" and help the children identify people they can turn to in their lives for help and advice.

E. Wrap-Up and Review of Folders

The leader distributes folders and says: "Remember that today is the last meeting that we will have together." When appropriate, the leader should invite the group to review the contents of the folders.

Clinical note: Note themes and ideas that may have recurred.

The leader should then share some of her or his feelings about the end of the group (e.g., having enjoyed the group, missing the group members in the future, believing in their futures, and, possibly, noting that it is difficult to say good-bye).

F. Awards

The leader distributes an award certificate to each child and notes that each award is different and personal. Each award certificate should be in an envelope or made private in some other way, and each child's award should reflect some positive quality in that child. The leader should attempt to reinforce authentic qualities, such as effort, bravery, or honesty. (Award certificates are available in stationery stores, on PowerPoint, or the example at the end of this session may be reproduced.)

G. Snack and Closure

The children are asked to sit around the table or in the original circle to get ready for the end of group. The leader asks each child what he or she wants, then distributes the snack. During snack time, it is a good idea to create a list of names and phone numbers for each child. The leader should make available the same number of blank sheets as there are children. Each child starts a list with his or her own name and number and then passes it to his or her neighbor. The children can each be asked to state one thing they will most miss about not coming to group and one thing that they will not miss. End the session at a clearly specified time.

H. Follow-Up

If the parents of the children in the group were not participating in their own parent group, then the leader distributes a letter to each parent at this time, listing whatever continuing services might be available to the children. The list should be as specific as possible; for example, if additional groups will be run, the leader should specify the dates and times (even if these are approximate). Names and phone numbers of individual counselors or agencies in the area should be included, with some reference to the fee schedule if possible. After the letter is distributed, the leader should follow up with a phone call or meeting with the parents, in which the leader provides individual recommendations for follow-up for each child.

The Turtle Story

Once upon a time, there was a sand turtle named Sammy. Sammy lived in the sand by the ocean, just near the edge of the woods. Every day he loved to lie in the sun on the sandy beach. He also liked to make tunnels and secret hideaways in the sand dunes. His favorite food was sand crabs. Nearby, in the ocean lived a sea turtle named Sally. Sally lived deep down in the ocean and loved to frolic and swim in the waves. She loved to feel the cool blue-green water on her body as she hunted for jellyfish to eat.

One day Sammy the sand turtle crawled to the water's edge to look for sand crabs. At the same time, Sally the sea turtle swam to the shallow part of the beach where she could poke her head out of the water to see the blue sky. All at once Sally's and Sammy's eyes met and they fell in love. Sally had never seen a sand turtle before, and she thought he looked different and handsome in his dark brown shell. Sammy had never seen a sea turtle before, and he thought Sally's blue-green shell was so different and just the prettiest he had ever seen.

The two turtles loved each other so much that they decided to get married. For a time they lived at the water's edge so that Sammy could sit on the sand and keep warm and dry while Sally sat in the shallow water to keep cool. Pretty soon they had two baby turtles named Tommy and Tina. These little baby turtles had very nice brown and blue-green shells. They looked something like each of their parents.

Tommy and Tina Turtle loved to play in the sand with their father, Sammy. They would spend hours digging tunnels and searching for sand crabs to eat. Sometimes they would take naps side by side in the warm sand. When they pulled in their heads and legs, their shells looked like rocks sticking halfway out of the sand. Tommy and Tina also loved to frolic in the sea with their mother, Sally. They did somersaults in the waves and explored the underwater caves and reefs, looking for jellyfish to eat. For a while this was a happy family of turtles.

But then something went wrong! Tommy and Tina Turtle were having so much fun that they didn't notice that Sammy, the father sand turtle, was spending less and less time at the water's edge. He wandered up into the sand dunes and hunted for food near the edge of the woods. Sally, the mother sea turtle, spent all her time swimming in the deep part of the ocean, and she did not sit in the shallow water on the beach anymore. Each night, when the father and mother turtles met to feed the kid turtles some dinner, they would argue and fight. Sometimes Sammy the sand turtle and Sally the sea turtle snapped at each other. Tommy and Tina were scared their parents might hurt each other. Sometimes the mother and father turtles refused to talk to each other. Sammy, the father sand turtle, would pull his head into his shell and dig into the sand, and Sally, the mother sea turtle, turned her back on him and dove into the ocean.

Alternative Ending 1 (Focus: Separation and Divorce)

[If parents are planning to separate or have separated, the story should continue here.]

One day, Sammy and Sally decided they didn't want to live together anymore. Sally decided to live at the bottom of the ocean, and Sammy decided to live up in the sand dunes above the beach.

Tommy and Tina Turtle were very sad. They were still young turtles and needed someone to look after them. They loved both their mom and their dad and wanted to be with both of them all the time. Tina was kind of angry, and she yelled a lot and had fights with her mom. Tommy was angry, too, but he kept his feelings inside and hid in his shell all day. He wouldn't even play with his sister or any of his friends. Most of all, Tommy and Tina Turtle wanted their parents to live together at the water's edge and to be a happy family again.

One day they decided to ask Wise Old Owl to help them. Wise Old Owl always gave good advice to all the animals, and she could fix almost any problem. Early the next morning they packed a picnic lunch and set off for the forest to look for Wise Old Owl. She was sleeping in a tree when they arrived, but she woke up and invited them into her tree stump for a visit. Very soon they told her the problem. Tina Turtle then asked, "Can you make our mother and father live together again?" Tommy Turtle said, "Please, please make them love each other again!"

Wise Old Owl stared thoughtfully into the sky for some time and then said: "It's very difficult for a sand turtle and a sea turtle to live together. They are two different kinds of turtles, and they need different kinds of homes. Sammy the sand turtle likes to dig in the sand and sit in the warm sun. Sally the sea turtle likes to dive down deep under the ocean waves and swim in the cool blue water. When they tried to live together at the water's edge, they were both unhappy, cross, and angry. It was too wet and cold for Sammy and too dry and hot for Sally. It is much better that they each live in the place where they can be happy and have the things around them that they need.

"But you, Tommy Turtle, and you, Tina Turtle, are each half sand turtle and half sea turtle. You can live in the cool ocean and eat jellyfish and you can live on the warm sand and eat sand crabs. You can have fun with your mother and you can also have fun with your father. They love you very much and they want you to be happy. The best plan is for you to live some of the time in the water with your mother and some of the time on land with your father."

And that is just what Tommy Turtle and Tina Turtle did! Sometimes they lived in the deep blue ocean and practiced their swimming with their mother and sometimes they lived on the warm, sunny sand and practiced hunting in the dunes near the woods with their father. They made lots of friends with all the fish and dolphins and whales in the ocean, and they made lots of friends with the deer and the badgers and the foxes that lived in the woods. They loved their mother and they loved their father. In fact, Tommy and Tina Turtle became happy again and grew up to be very special turtles, with beautiful brownish-bluish-green-colored shells that were remarkably fine looking and exceptionally sturdy. Wise Old Owl said this was probably because they had made the best of living in two different worlds, and everyone agreed that this was so.

Alternative Ending 2 (Focus: Ongoing Conflict or Violence)

Clinical note: The leader may make further modifications or additions (including creating a synthesis of both alternative endings) to meet the needs and experiences of the group participants.

Sammy, the father sand turtle, would pull his head into his shell and dig into the sand, and Sally, the mother sea turtle, turned her back on him and dove into the ocean waves. This went on for a long time, and it was hard for Tommy and Tina to bear. Tina got kind of angry and yelled a lot and had fights with other kids and with Tommy. Tommy was angry, too, but he kept his feelings inside and hid in his shell a lot of the time. Most of all, Tommy and Tina wanted the fighting to stop.

One day the young turtles decided to ask Wise Old Owl to help them. Wise Old Owl always gave good advice to all the animals, and she could fix almost any problem. Early the next morning they packed a picnic lunch and set off for the forest to look for Wise Old Owl. She was sleeping in a tree when they arrived, but she woke up and invited them in to her tree for a visit. Very soon they told her the problem, and Tommy Turtle said, "Please, please make them stop fighting and love each other again!"

Wise Old Owl stared thoughtfully into the sky for some time and then said: "It's very difficult for a sand turtle and a sea turtle to live together. They are two very different kinds of turtles, who need very different things. They might learn how to stop fighting, but they will certainly need help from someone who is wise. They can come to me or to another owl in my family if they want, but they have to make the journey themselves. Neither you, Tina, nor you, Tommy, can do it for them, no matter how much you may want to help.

"If there is a lot of fighting, you might want to go to your neighbors the seagulls, or your friends the badgers, or the blue dolphins for help from animals who are big and strong. You might need to go inside your shells to stay safe some of the time, but you don't have to stay there all the time. Remember, there are other things that young turtles like to do and can do. You, Tommy Turtle, and you, Tina Turtle, are each half sand turtle and half sea turtle. You can live in the cool ocean and eat jellyfish and you can live on the warm sand and eat sand crabs. You can live your own lives in peace. You can love your mother and your father and still want to have a different kind of life when you grow up. You can make a solemn promise to yourselves that when you become grown-up turtles, with beautiful brownish-bluish-green-colored shells, you will make families of your very own where no one needs to feel afraid."

Tommy and Tina felt that this was good advice. They were very, very quiet for a long time. They could hear the birds singing in the forest and feel the sun shining down. Then, without saying anything, Tina walked quietly up to Wise Old Owl and said, "Owl, will you hear my promise and keep it for me until I am big?" The owl nodded; she understood that this was very, very important. Then Tina bowed her head and took a deep breath and said, "I, Tina Turtle, do solemnly promise that I will grow up and make a peaceful family, where no one needs to be afraid. I will always remember how sad and mad the fighting makes me feel now. The memory of these feelings and the owl will help me to always remember my promise." Tina sighed a big sigh. She felt better and stronger than she had ever felt. Then it was Tommy's turn. He too went up to Wise Old Owl and said, "I, Tommy Turtle, do solemnly promise that I will grow up and make a peaceful family, where no one needs to be afraid. I will always remember how sad and mad the fighting makes me feel now. The memory of these feelings and the owl will help me to always remember my promise." Tommy sighed and smiled at Tina. He too felt stronger now. Then they thanked Wise Old Owl and began the rest of their lives.

Sometimes they played in the deep blue ocean and practiced their swimming with their mother, and sometimes they spent time on the warm, sunny sand and practiced hunting in the dunes near the woods with their father. Sometimes they all did things together. Those were good times. Sally and Sammy learned how to work things out some of the time. Sometimes they still had fights. Those were not such good times. When this happened, Tommy and Tina stayed together and mostly kept their heads in their shells, which was very smart of them. Sometimes they would go swimming in the ocean or running in the forest to get out some of the mad feelings. Every once in a while they got help from seagulls or dolphins, which was also very smart of them. When they got older they went out swimming or hunting with their friends, and that made life feel very good. Tommy and Tina grew up to be very special turtles who remembered their promise to Wise Old Owl all their lives long. They were remarkably fine looking, exceptionally sturdy, and, most of all, they were peaceful and unafraid.

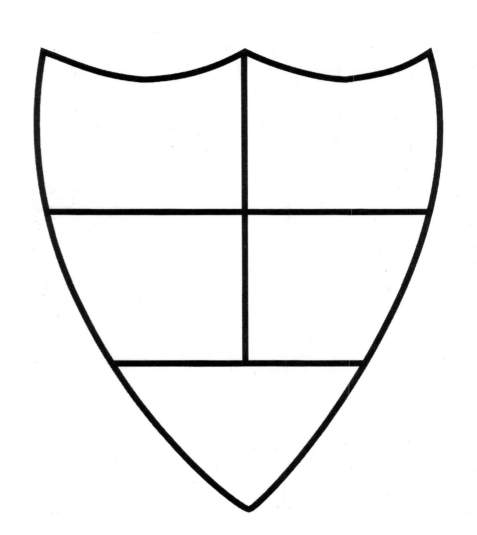

Certificate of Distinction

in Recognition of

For Distinguished Achievement in

PART III:
APPENDIXES

Appendix A

Troubleshooting for Both LK and BK Groups

STRATEGIES FOR PREVENTING MANAGEMENT DIFFICULTIES

Evaluate and Balance Groups

Use intake and screening to do the following:

1. Identify children with well-documented histories of acting out in groups. The leader will need to decide if enough resources (coleaders, extra time for planning or holding conferences) are available to manage this child in the group. If not, the child is not a good candidate.
2. Identify, to the degree possible, an optimal balance of boys to girls and a mix of life experiences and personalities.
3. Identify the issues that the children are concerned with. This will help the leader to identify the right mix of children who have similar histories as well as pictures, activities, and questions that will keep the children involved.
4. Decide whether the group will need one or more leaders. When in doubt, and another leader is available, it is best to use two leaders because it is difficult to predict how the children will react.

Pick the Right Group Room

Sometimes there will be no choice about the room, but it is important to work thoughtfully with what is available.

1. Try to make the room a protected place. People who are not in the group should not be able to come in or hover around the group room during group.
2. Limit distractions. Cover windows, unplug phones, remove toys that are not used in group, keep snack out of room until snack time.

3. Try to use a table and chairs for structured activities, as well as a rug area for unstructured activities.

Prepare Carefully Before Every Session

All leader instructions to the group are designed to be said in your own words, so it is important to be very familiar with what is to be communicated. Also, it may be necessary to substitute activities or stimulus pictures for role-plays that are more relevant to the needs of the particular group. All of this takes planning. Groups quickly lose focus when the leader is unprepared or must pause to find materials.

Provide materials to keep hands busy during discussion or sharing:

Crayons and pictures from coloring books or plain paper can be available for children to color with.
Modeling beeswax can be available for shaping.
Yarn can be available for finger knitting.

STRATEGIES FOR MANAGEMENT WHEN THE GROUP IS UNFOCUSED OR OUT OF CONTROL

Use a Seating Plan

Use a fixed seating plan at the group table to help separate children who distract each other. The plan should be flexible—change it as necessary. When the group is losing focus, have them return to their seats. At that point it may be useful to begin a silent activity.

Change the Atmosphere

The leader can dim some of the lights or lower his or her voice until the group refocuses.

Move Ahead to Videotaping

Set up a rule that the camera goes on only when there is calm, otherwise the group is wasting time and film. When that expectation is in place, the group will often calm down because they want to go on camera.

Change the Content to Keep it Relevant

If stimulus pictures for role-plays do not capture the concerns or cultural realities of the children in the group, use different ones that do. See pages 24-25 for a discussion of how this can be done. Photographs may be found in news magazines. (Be careful not to use material that is more violent or frightening than anything the children may have referred to.) Photos that *suggest* the children's concerns are preferable (e.g., police officers entering or leaving a house is preferable to police using weapons or restraints). Pictures may be found in books for children. Examples include the following:

1. People who are sick
2. People (adults or peers) with guns or knives
3. People (adults or peers) physically fighting
4. Police entering a home
5. Police taking a family member out of a home
6. Families being evicted
7. Families being separated

Slow Down When Children Are Having a Hard Time Understanding What to Do

When children are immature or highly traumatized, they may be very concrete. Many of the ideas in the sessions will be new. Keep the instructions very simple and use a lot of demonstration. Use activities for the younger groups and even with older groups.

Get Active When the Children Seem Bored

The leader can pick up the pace by limiting sharing and discussion and going to the active part of the work more quickly.

Change the Intensity Level to Limit Anxiety

The group may become restless and distractible because the material is raising too much anxiety. The leader may need to shift to a more controlled way of working:

1. Work silently. Many of the activities can be done without any words, as charades. This provides greater control and containment.
2. Work with puppets. Many of the activities can be done with puppets. This provides more distance and can prevent the children from becoming flooded with too much feeling.

Use a Token Economy

Screening information may help the leader to determine ahead of time whether this kind of management is necessary, or it can be introduced after the group begins. Rules include the following:

1. At the beginning of group, each child receives a regular snack coupon and two tokens. Regular snack coupons can never be taken away. All children receive regular snack unconditionally.
2. Bonus tokens are used to purchase additional snack items at the end of each session. Each additional snack item is worth two bonus tokens.
3. Leader awards bonus tokens to children who are working hard and following the rules, to a maximum of four tokens per session.
4. If children repeatedly violate group rules, it may be necessary to add a consequence to the token economy.
5. For specific violations of group rules, the leader may give one warning and then take a bonus token away.
6. The child may earn it back or purchase half a snack item if she or he is left with one bonus token.
7. Remember, the regular snack coupon is never taken away.

STRATEGIES FOR HELPING INDIVIDUAL CHILDREN STAY FOCUSED AND IN CONTROL

Time-Out

See a discussion of time-out in the Little Kids' Manual, page 97. Remember that if a child needs to be removed from the group, it should only be for a very brief amount of time and done with a coleader, who can stay with the child and help him or her to calm down and return to the group. These children are likely to become panicked about being abandoned if they are left alone.

Stay Close

Allow a coleader to stay close to a child who is having trouble; a gentle hand on the back or shoulder can sometimes bring calm and help the child to know that an adult is there to contain him or her.

Provide Special Responsibilities

Some children have a particular capacity to lead their peers into distractions. Such a child's potential leadership abilities can sometimes be redirected. He or she may be given specific, limited responsibilities for assisting the leader in performing tasks such as distributing and collecting materials, taking charge of a timer for timing, or selling snacks if a token economy is being used. This strategy of assigning specific tasks to a disruptive child should not be confused with allowing overburdened or caretaking children to assume leadership tasks.

Meet with the Child's Parents

Set up a conference with the child's parents to decide if it is possible for her or him to continue in group. If it is decided that the child will continue, develop a behavioral contract. Use positive-reinforcement techniques in the contract whenever possible.

If a Child Must Be Expelled from Group

Removing a child from group is always a last resort, but it is sometimes necessary. When this happens, it is important for the leader to explain the reasons why the child could no longer be in group in terms that are neutral, respectful, and compassionate. The other children will need time to talk about their feelings as soon as possible. They may wish to write the child a group letter of support in order to create closure.

STRATEGIES FOR PRESERVING GROUP SAFETY

If a Child Is Accidentally Hurt

The leader has a serious responsibility to ensure that group is safe and controlled. Still, it is not always possible to avoid accidental injuries when children are involved in boisterous activity. If this happens, it is important for the leader to keep in mind how anxious these children are likely to become about this momentary loss of safety. They will need to see that the leader handles the situation calmly and that the injury is carefully nursed. If another child is responsible for the injury, the leader can use the episode as an opportunity to help him or her to acknowledge responsibility and make appropriate amends (e.g., helping to fix the injury, making an apology) without losing face.

When a Child Becomes too Aggressive in the Role-Play

A child may get so involved in an aggressive role that he or she may seem frighteningly out of control to the other children. When this happens, the leader must intervene immediately to preserve the sense of safety in group. The leader can have the child freeze in role and allow the other role players to identify their feelings and the feelings that they read in the aggressive child's body posture and face. For example, the leader may say, "Okay, Tommy, let's freeze that for the camera and find out how it looks to your audience." This needs to be done with care. This is not an attack but an opportunity for an aggressive child to notice his or her impact on others. The aggressive child can then be empowered by new directions. The leader can say, for example, "Let's take the action down a notch, and see how it looks" or "Let's say, in the role-play, that you noticed the others were scared, how would that change the action? Let's see that."

When a Child Offers a Fantasy of Violent Revenge in a Follow-Up Role-Play

This represents an opportunity for the leader to notice the strong feelings that are the basis of the fantasy. The feelings must be acknowledged. The leader can then discuss, in matter-of-fact terms, what would happen if the fantasy were actually acted out, what rules of moral conduct would be violated, what the consequences for the child would be, and so on. The leader can identify the negative consequences to the child in a supportive way and also help the group to look at the difference between feeling solutions and real-world solutions that lead to enhanced coping.

STRATEGIES FOR ADDRESSING ISSUES IN INDIVIDUAL TREATMENT

Distrustful, Avoidant Children

Help the child to make the avoidance concrete, so she or he can work with it in therapy. To do so, encourage hide-and-seek games in the therapy room or in the sand tray, using masks, sunglasses, screens, tunnels, barricades, and other hiding places. Allow the child to build a secret place that can be entered only at his or her invitation. A variation of Blind Walk (BK Session 2,B) may be appropriate. Also Inside Me/Outside Me (BK Session 7,D) and Masks and Role-Plays (BK Session 7,E) can be useful.

Anxious, Controlling Children

Allow the child as much control as possible in order to reduce his or her anxiety and need for distance. Allow him or her to sit in the therapist's chair. Ask permission for any intervention that is made. Negotiate the agenda for the session, allowing plenty of room for activities that provide respite from the work. Use guided imagery and other relaxation techniques such as "smell the cookies, blow out the candles" or tight/loose muscles.

Concrete, Dispirited Children Who Cannot Use Fantasy

In general, it is useful to treat these very constricted children as if they were younger than their actual age. Begin with concrete work that orients the child in time and place. Identify the details of a visitation schedule and make a calendar, discussing who lives where, including pets. Make a time line with the child that shows a chronology of important events in his or her life, including people that have come and gone, age at divorce or remarriage, and so on. Draw a family tree and describe who is related to whom. Use A Fantasy Room (BK Session 3,C) and related activities (BK Sessions 4-9) to help the child toward more self-awareness. Use List of Feelings (BK Session 1) and Feelings/Color (BK Session 1), and Level of Feelings (BK Session 2) and Charade of Feelings (BK Session 2), to help to make feelings seem less overwhelming. Jobs for People in Your Family (BK Session 5) may also be appropriate.

Children Who Engage in Repetitive Play Sequences

This can happen when children cannot find release from rigid ideas, rules, and expectations about the way relationships work. The therapist may choose to interpret the child's feeling of being stuck or intervene directly by suggesting different directions or endings to the play. If the child rejects the intervention, the therapist can ask why these endings are not possible. The never-ending quality of the play may reflect the never-ending quality of the family conflict. If this is so, the child's reality must be acknowledged within the play or directly interpreted.

Children Who Become Frightened and Disrupt Their Own Play and Fantasy

The therapist will need to help the child to modulate and slow down the play. Provide soothing, nonarousing alternatives (e.g., card or board games, throwing a ball through hoops) to help calm the child after a disruption.

(Note carefully what content the child disrupts, because it is likely to be diagnostic of central fears and conflicts.)

Children Who Become Overwhelmed, Regressed, or Out of Control

Use smaller play equipment requiring finer motor coordination. Use figures (e.g., animals, not people) to create more distance. Encourage the child to take control of the out-of-control actors and animals in their play. Help the child to identify the rules and become the director, the king, Superman. Help the child to bring in army or police figures to quell a riot. Remind the child of the rules of the playroom when it is necessary or as a way to provide reassurance. It is better to predict and avoid the child's escalation to the point of being overwhelmed if at all possible.

Appendix B

Psychoeducational Groups for Parents

The lasting value of the children's experiences in group depends in large part on the effectiveness of collateral work with their parents. Here the goals are to heighten the parents' capacity to perceive and respond to their children's needs separately from their own and enhance their motivation to make decisions and agreements that protect the children from further conflict, chaos, and abuse. These goals can be addressed quite effectively when the children's group leader also convenes psychoeducational groups for parents at intervals during the program. In this format, the leader can provide the parents with information about the effects of family conflict and violence in general and then translate these general issues into more specific concerns of individual children. In a sense, the meetings resemble group parent-teacher conferences in which the teacher (leader) describes the curriculum as it pertains to the needs of the class (group) and then focuses on the strengths and weaknesses of the individual student. In the psychoeducational group, as in the parent-teacher conference, it is the leader's direct experience of the child that makes her or him credible to the parent. In this dual role, it is important that the leader protect the children's confidentiality. In general, this means that the leader is free to discuss her or his impressions of the child's needs, concerns, and coping style but does not directly quote the child or share writings or drawings that are produced in group without the child's permission.

Psychoeducational group meetings may be convened at the beginning, in the middle, and toward the end of the children's program (which involves weekly sessions over a ten- to twelve-week period). In order to maximize parents' attendance, the meetings can be scheduled to follow the children's sessions, and child care is provided. Scheduling also permits highly conflicted or violent parents to participate separately. A child's father, for example, might attend parent group meetings scheduled for the first, fifth, and ninth weeks of the program, while the child's mother might attend during the second, sixth, and tenth weeks.

The work begins with education. Here the leader establishes the commonality of the parents' experience with chronic conflict and abuse and provides information about its effects on children in general. A working metaphor can provide an effective framework for understanding. For example, the child's sense of self can be likened to a tapestry that cannot be woven into a whole design without the horizontal (mother) and vertical (father) strands to hold it in place. Even when one or both strands are of poor quality, they cannot be ripped away without unraveling the whole design. Instead, the design itself must be strengthened. Once this kind of working frame of reference is in place, the leader describes subtle signs of distress in school-age children and explains why some youngsters seem to show no signs at all. This explanation focuses on how children learn to "keep from unraveling inside" or to function "as double agents in a militarized zone," becoming guarded and overcontrolled in their efforts to maintain appearances and predict what will be required of them. Here the leader particularly emphasizes the ways in which children's efforts to achieve safety and control can leave them feeling as if they are not completely real and thus they are unable to form authentic relationships. With this information on the table, the leader can begin to help parents to understand how these coping efforts can undermine children's self-esteem and limit their ability to mature in their understanding of themselves, other people, and relationships. This provides a foundation for explaining how a working agreement between parents can support the children by providing a predictable environment that protects their children's involvement in life beyond the conflict and outside the family.

Once the leader has communicated these general points, the individual children become the focus of discussion. The leader frames his or her comments as observations that the parent is invited to confirm or interpret differently. In a discussion of the children's need to maintain appearances, for example, the leader may say, "I've noticed that both Jane and John try really hard to get things perfectly right. It seems as if it's difficult for them to take risks. For instance, one of them had trouble making a drawing without a ruler and lots of erasing. I wonder if it's difficult for them to make mistakes. Do you (either parent) notice this in your child? What do you make of it?" This approach can help the parent to focus on the child without undermining his or her parental authority or competence. Parents' responses to these kinds of questions often lead to discussions of the causes of the child's difficulties. Some parents begin to see themselves and their role in the conflict more clearly when they recognize themselves in the points of view of others. Others benefit from feedback that group members provide with a kind of directness and authority that comes from shared experience. When this happens, it is the leader's responsibility to maintain a safe and constructive tone in the group discussion. Throughout the parent meetings, the leader also helps the parents to anticipate and support the kinds of changes that take place in the children as they work in group. This is particularly important because a number of children do become more curious, assertive, and even rebellious as they find their own voice. These shifts can be difficult for parents to understand, tolerate, and manage appropriately without information and direction from the group leader.

For some parents the experience in the psychoeducational group is enough to leverage their disengagement from the conflict and their commitment to developing and honoring coparenting agreements. This kind of outcome depends on the capacity of the parents to assimilate information about their child as an individual and to gain insight into their own roles in the conflict. More vulnerable parents generally benefit in a more circumscribed way, achieving (though not always maintaining) a limited degree of insight and a conceptual framework for understanding conflict and its effects.

For parents and other primary caretakers who need more extensive help with coparenting their children without chronic conflict and threat of violence, a more extensive therapeutic group intervention may be needed. This model is documented fully in Johnston, J.R. and Campbell, L. (1988). *Impasses of Divorce: The Dynamics and Resolution of Family Conflict* (New York: Free Press); and in Johnston, J.R. (1999). *Developing and Testing a Group Intervention for Families at Impasse.* Final report submitted to the State-Wide Office of Family Court Services, Judicial Council of the State of California, San Francisco (available from the author).

Briefly, in this more extensive intervention both parents or primary caretakers are generally referred from the family and dependency courts, some to attend voluntarily and some mandated to attend by court order. Following individual intake sessions, with each parent and child seen separately to obtain a history of the disputes and the child's experience of loss and trauma, groups of five to eight families are formed and seen in a series of eight weekly meetings.

During the first four sessions, parents (often accompanied by their new partners and extended family members) are seen separately in concurrent small groups. During this time they are successively invited to describe their children, identify their impasses to cooperative parenting, develop awareness about how their conflict affects their child, and clarify goals to be accomplished in resolving their difficulties. During the last four sessions, parents meet together in one large group to hear feedback on their children's dilemmas from the children's group leaders, practice communication and negotiation skills, and begin to mediate their differences. These groups are staffed by two experienced family counselors, preferably a male-female team who are ethnically diverse. Individual follow-up mediation and help with implementing agreements is then made available. It is important to note, however, that where there is serious threat of violence between parents they are not seen together but continue to be counseled in separate concurrent sessions, at different times and locations.

Appendix C

An Evaluation Study of the Group Model

The group interventions, commonly known as Children's Wellbeing Groups, were implemented and evaluated in three family service agency sites and five elementary schools in the San Francisco Bay Area.[1] Sites were chosen because of the high-risk neighborhoods they served and because they also offered a range of family counseling, advocacy, and referral services to families. Baseline and follow-up data were collected from at least two of the three sources (clinicians, teachers, and parents) and were available for 223 children, 106 girls and 117 boys (aged five to fourteen years).

Eligibility for the Wellbeing Groups included children who had

1. witnessed violence or been the object of violence (at home, in the neighborhood, or at school);
2. experienced highly conflicted marriages and litigated divorce (in which parents were hostile, verbally abusive, fearful, and highly distrustful of each other);
3. suffered the precipitous loss of a primary caregiver as a consequence of violence, abuse, or criminal behavior (by death, desertion, incarceration, parental abduction, deportation); and
4. been exposed to abusive and neglectful environments due to parents' or other adults' substance abuse.

All types of abuse except direct sexual abuse were included. However, the groups were not regarded as appropriate for severely emotionally disturbed and behaviorally uncontrollable children.

Children were identified through a variety of extant referral networks within the schools and agency sites. Referral sources included judges, mediators, teachers, school counselors, principals, therapists, advocates, and parents or legal guardians. The primary custodial caretaker gave permission for each child's participation and agreed to provide data at intake interviews and about six months later. In addition, parents, guardians and foster parents, grandparents, and other relatives were invited to attend parent groups, held monthly at most sites (some of the school sites offered weekly parent support groups). Those adults who had been abusive met in separate groups from their victims.

Group Composition

On average, seven children attended each group series. Each series comprised ten weekly meetings, each 90 minutes long, at the family agency sites; at the school sites, the meetings occurred over one semester, or fifteen weeks, each almost one hour in duration. The groups were composed of children of similar grade level and same age range (five- to seven-year-olds; eight- to eleven-year-olds, and twelve- to fourteen-year-olds). The groups were usually led by two clinicians: one a trained and experienced counselor and one a student counselor. However, when short-staffed, groups were conducted by one experienced counselor in some sites. One bilingual/bicultural counselor participated at each school site, where groups were often conducted concurrently in English and Spanish.

Attendance

Attendance at the children's group sessions averaged 85 percent. The school sites tended to have slightly better attendance (89 percent) compared to the agency sites (80 percent). Parent involvement in the program was less than anticipated. Attendance at parent groups varied widely across settings and over time, with about one-half of parents participating at least once during the series. Generally, a small group of four to five parents attended regularly.

Demographic Descriptors

The families were of multiethnic origin, the two largest groups being Caucasian (42 percent) and Hispanic (36 percent). African Americans comprised 10 percent, and other racial groups made up 12 percent of the sample. Socioeconomic status of the families was obtained from indirect measures since income data were not available. Three-fourths of parents had obtained no more than a high school education; 42 percent received government welfare benefits (MediCal), and 23 percent received Victims of Crime (VOC) funding.

The children were predominantly from single-parent families (80 percent). It was equally likely that parents had never married, were separated, or were already divorced. Parents who were currently married and still living together were the minority (20 percent). Mothers were the primary caretakers of the children in 58 percent of cases. Foster parents, grandparents, and other relatives cared for 15 percent of the children.

The overwhelming majority (87 percent) of the children had experienced separation and loss in their family; 70 percent had been exposed to both domestic violence and child abuse or neglect issues, and almost half (43 percent) had family members in trouble with the law. Substance abuse by a household member and neighborhood violence had affected 36 percent and 32 percent, respectively. Half of the children had been exposed to multiple types of traumatic events, and one-fourth had suffered at least five of the six types of events (separation/loss, neighborhood violence, domestic violence, parent-child difficulties, substance abuse, and trouble with the law).

Program Evaluation

After the group intervention and at a six-month follow-up, according to clinicians' and teachers' ratings on standardized measures, children who received the group intervention showed significantly increased social competence compared to baseline.[2] Parents and clinicians also perceived significantly fewer emotional and behavioral problems in the youngsters over the study period. Boys generally had more problematic behavior at the outset but made similar improvement compared to girls. In sum, the overall findings on all measures were uniformly positive; the effects were modest to substantial in size and statistically significant. Qualitative comments from teachers and clinicians confirmed the children's progress. Children identified because of difficulties getting along with peers, poor capacity for empathy with others, limited problem-solving skills, and a tendency to erupt into violence were noted, after the group intervention, to have a greater capacity to express their feelings and ideas in appropriate ways and a more mature understanding of interpersonal relationships.

Furthermore, the group interventions were assessed as economically feasible. It was estimated that the group program costs only 43 percent of what a similar number of hours of individual therapy would cost. That is, on average it costs twelve counselor contact hours for each child seen within groups, whereas individual sessions for a similar length of time would cost twenty eight counselor contact hours. In fact, these groups were self-sustaining on a combination of MediCal and VOC funding in schools, both of which were supplemented by low sliding-scale fees in agency settings. There is a critical need to provide low-cost preventive mental health services for broad populations of at-risk children, and it appears that group interventions may be the only way in which this can be achieved.

Notes

Introduction

1. Roseby, V. and Johnston, J.R. (1997). *High-Conflict, Violent, and Separating Families: A Group Treatment Manual for School-Age Children.* New York: Free Press.

2. For example, Grotzky, L., Camerer, C., and Damiano, L. (2000). *Group Work with Sexually Abused Children: A Practitioner's Guide.* Thousand Oaks, CA: Sage.

3. Johnston, J.R., Gans Walters, M., and Olesen, N.W. (in review). The Psychological Functioning of Alienated Children in Custody Disputing Families: An Exploratory Study. *Journal of Forensic Psychiatry & Psychology.*

4. Ibid.

LK Session 1

1. See pp. 90-94 for information about the puppets.

Appendix C

1. For a full report of the study see Johnston, J.R. (2003). Group Interventions for Children At-Risk from Abuse and Witness to Violence: A Report of a Study. *Journal of Emotional Abuse,* 3(3/4): 203-226.

2. Teachers and group leaders completed the Teaching-Child Rating Scale (TRS): Hightower, A.D., Work, W.C., Cowen, E.L., Lotyczewski, B.S., Spinell, A.P., Guare, J.C., and Rohrbeck, C.A. (1986). The Teacher-Child Rating Scale: A Brief Objective Measure of Elementary Children's School Problem Behaviors and Competencies. *School Psychology Review,* 15: 393-409; and parents completed the Child Behavior Checklist (CBCL): Achenbach, T.M. and Edelbrock, C. (1983). *Manual for the Child Behavior Checklist and Revised Child Behavior Profile.* Burlington, VT: Queen City Printers.

Bibliography

This bibliography contains therapeutic stories for children who experience family disruption and/or trauma.

Alcoholism

Carrick, Carol (1995). *Banana Beer*. Niles, IL: Albert Whitman.
Thomas, Jane Resh (1996). *Daddy Doesn't Have to Be a Giant Anymore*. New York: Clarion Books.

Divorce and Single-Parent Families

Brown, Laurene Krasny and Marc Brown (1986). *Dinosaurs Divorce: A Guide for Changing Families*. New York: Little, Brown and Company.
Johnston, Janet, Karen Breunig, Carla Garrity, and Mitchell Baris (1997). *Through the Eyes of Children: Healing Stories for Children of Divorce*. New York: Free Press.
Tax, Meredith (1981). *Families*. New York: The Feminist Press at the City University of New York.

Domestic Violence and Anger Management

Bernstein, Sharon Chesler (1991). *A Family That Fights*. Morton Grove, IL: Albert Whitman.
Whitehouse, Elain and Warwick Pudney (1996). *A Volcano in My Tummy: Helping Children to Handle Anger*. New Society Publishers, P.O. Box 189, Gabriola Island, B.C. VOR IXO, Canada.

Geographical Dislocation and Homelessness

Soman, David (1992). *The Leaving Morning*. New York: Orchard Books.
Testa, Maria (1996). *Someplace to Go*. Morton Grove, IL: Albert Whitman.

Incarceration of Parent

Gesme, Carole (1993). *Help for Kids: Understanding Your Feelings About Having a Parent in Prison or Jail.* Minneapolis, MN: Pine Press. (Also available through the Pacific Oaks Clearinghouse.)

Hickman, Martha Whitmore (1990). *When Andy's Father Went to Prison.* Niles, IL: Albert Whitman.

Rosenkarantz, Louise (1984). *I Know How You Feel, Because This Happened to Me: A Handbook for Kids with a Parent in Prison.* Prison Match, 2121 Russel St., Berkeley, CA 94705.

Loss and Grief

Brown, Laurie Krasny and Marc Brown (1996). *When Dinosaurs Die: A Guide to Understanding Death.* New York: Little, Brown and Company.

Palmer, Pat (1994). *"I Wish I Could Hold Your Hand . . .": A Child's Guide to Grief and Loss.* Impact Publishers, Inc., PO Box 6016, Atascadero, CA 93423-6016.

Separation and Foster Care

Lanners, Karen and Ken Schwartzenberger (unpublished). Therapeutic Stories for Children in Foster Care. C/o Family Care Network, 508 Higuera St., San Luis Obispo, CA 93401. (805) 781-3535.

Sexual Abuse

Davis, Nancy (1988). *Once Upon a Time . . . : Therapeutic Stories to Heal Abused Children.* Distributed by Self-Esteem Shop, 4607 N. Woodward, Royal Oak, MI 48073.

Girard, Linda Walvoord (1984). *My Body Is Private.* Morton Grove, IL: Albert Whitman.

Index

Page numbers followed by the letter "i" indicate illustrations.

THE HAWORTH MALTREATMENT AND TRAUMA PRESS®
Robert A. Geffner, PhD
Senior Editor

THE SOCIALLY SKILLED CHILD MOLESTER: DIFFERENTIATING THE GUILTY FROM THE FALSELY ACCUSED by Carla van Dam. (2006).

A SAFE PLACE TO GROW: A GROUP TREATMENT MANUAL FOR CHILDREN IN CONFLICTED, VIOLENT, AND SEPARATING HOMES by Vivienne Roseby, Janet Johnston, Bettina Gentner, and Erin Moore. (2005). "This superb book captures the suffering, the bewilderment, and the hypervigilance of children who have witnessed parental fighting or have themselves been victims of violence, providing the clinician with new ways to restore the developmental processes that have been disrupted in these children and their families." *Judith Wallerstein, PhD, Divorce Researcher, Author of* The Unexpected Legacy of Divorce; *Founder of the Judith Wallerstein Center for the Family in Transition*

ON THE GROUND AFTER SEPTEMBER 11: MENTAL HEALTH RE-SPONSES AND PRACTICAL KNOWLEDGE GAINED edited by Yael Danieli and Robert L. Dingman. (2005). "A must-read for disaster planners as well as the many agencies that respond to large-scale mass fatality events. The variety of experiences shared prove the need for close collaboration and coordination before an event occurs in order to initiate and manage an effective response." *Dusty Bowenkamp, RN, CTS, Senior Associate (Ret.), American Red Cross, Disaster Mental Health Services*

CHILD TRAUMA HANDBOOK: A GUIDE FOR HELPING TRAUMA-EXPOSED CHILDREN AND ADOLESCENTS by Ricky Greenwald. (2005). "This is a fascinating book on how to respectfully approach and treat traumatized children. But it is so much more; it shows how to build on underlying health and strengths in both children and their caretakers. It is an empowering book and a well of clinical wisdom in a user-friendly step-by-step frame." *Atle Dyregrov, PhD, Founder, Center for Crisis Psychology, Bergen, Norway*

DEPRESSION IN NEW MOTHERS: CAUSES, CONSEQUENCES, AND TREATMENT ALTERNATIVES by Kathleen A. Kendall-Tackett. (2005). "Without a doubt, this book is a must-read for anyone working with childbearing women. The mothers we serve deserve nothing less than knowledgeable, prepared practitioners." *Karin Cadwell, PhD, RN, FAAN, IBCLC, Faculty, Healthy Children Project, East Sandwich, Massachusetts; Adjunct Faculty, The Union Institute & University, Cincinnati, Ohio*

EFFECTS OF AND INTERVENTIONS FOR CHILDHOOD TRAUMA FROM INFANCY THROUGH ADOLESCENCE: PAIN UNSPEAKABLE by Sandra B. Hutchison. (2005). "Insightful, provocative, informative, and resourceful. This book needs to be in the hands of all professionals working with children, preparting to work with children, or considering work with children. It illustrates the many faces of trauma and illuminates the many responses of children to trauma." *Osofo Calvin Banks, MDiv, Founder and Facilitator, Sesa Woruban Center for Spiritual Development; Certified Supervisor, Association for Clinical and Pastoral Education, Inc.*

MOTHER-DAUGHTER INCEST: A GUIDE FOR HELPING PROFESSIONALS by Beverly A. Ogilvie. (2004). "Beverly A. Ogilvie has succeeded in writing what will become the definitive resource for therapists working with mother-daughter incest....This book will be an invaluable tool for anyone working with this population." *Gina M. Pallotta, PhD, Licensed Psychologist; Associate Professor of Psychology and Clinical Graduate Director, California State University, Stanislaus*

MUNCHAUSEN BY PROXY: IDENTIFICATION, INTERVENTION, AND CASE MANAGEMENT by Louisa J. Lasher and Mary S. Sheridan. (2004). "This book is an excellent resource for professionals from all disciplines who may be confronted with this misunderstood disorder....This book is a must for every professional involved in MBP investigations." *Larry C. Brubaker, MA, FBI Special Agent (Retired)*

SCHIZOPHRENIA: INNOVATIONS IN DIAGNOSIS AND TREATMENT by Colin A. Ross. (2004). "Well-documented and clearly explained ... has hugely significant implications for our diagnostic system and for how severely disturbed people are understood and treated." *John Read, PhD, Editor,* Models of Madness: Psychological, Social, and Biological Approaches to Schizophrenia; *Director of Clinical Psychology, The University of Auckland, New Zealand*

REBUILDING ATTACHMENTS WITH TRAUMATIZED CHILDREN: HEALING FROM LOSSES, VIOLENCE, ABUSE, AND NEGLECT by Richard Kagan. (2004). "Dr. Richard Kagan, a recognized expert in working with traumatized children, has written a truly impressive book. Not only does the book contain a wealth of information for understanding the complex issues faced by traumatized youngsters, but it also offers specific interventions that can be used to help these children and their caregivers become more hopeful and resilient. . . . I am certain that this book will be read and reread by professionals engaged in improving the lives of at-risk youth." *Robert Brooks, PhD, Faculty, Harvard Medical School and author of* Raising Resilient Children *and* The Power of Resilience

PSYCHOLOGICAL TRAUMA AND THE DEVELOPING BRAIN: NEUROLOGICALLY BASED INTERVENTIONS FOR TROUBLED CHILDREN by Phyllis T. Stien and Joshua C. Kendall. (2003). "Stien and Kendall provide us with a great service. In this clearly written and important book, they synthesize a wealth of crucial information that links childhood trauma to brain abnormalities and subsequent mental illness. Equally important, they show us how the trauma also affects the child's social and intellectual development. I recommend this book to all clinicians and administrators." *Charles L. Whitfield, MD, Author of* The Truth About Depression *and* The Truth About Mental Illness

CHILD MALTREATMENT RISK ASSESSMENTS: AN EVALUATION GUIDE by Sue Righthand, Bruce Kerr, and Kerry Drach. (2003). "This book is essential reading for clinicians and forensic examiners who see cases involving issues related to child maltreatment. The authors have compiled an impressive critical survey of the relevant research on child maltreatment. Their material is well organized into sections on definitions, impact, risk assessment, and risk management. This book represents a giant step toward promoting evidence-based evaluations, treatment, and testimony." *Diane H. Schetky, MD, Professor of Psychiatry, University of Vermont College of Medicine*

SIMPLE AND COMPLEX POST-TRAUMATIC STRESS DISORDER: STRATEGIES FOR COMPREHENSIVE TREATMENT IN CLINICAL PRACTICE edited by Mary Beth Williams and John F. Sommer Jr. (2002). "A welcome addition to the literature on treating survivors of traumatic events, this volume possesses all the ingredients necessary for even the experienced clinician to master the management of patients with PTSD." *Terence M. Keane, PhD, Chief, Psychology Service, VA Boston Healthcare System; Professor and Vice Chair of Research in Psychiatry, Boston University School of Medicine*

FOR LOVE OF COUNTRY: CONFRONTING RAPE AND SEXUAL HARASSMENT IN THE U.S. MILITARY by T. S. Nelson. (2002). "Nelson brings an important message—that the absence of current media attention doesn't mean the problem has gone away; that only decisive action by military leadership at all levels can break the cycle of repeated traumatization; and that the failure to do so is, as Nelson puts it, a 'power failure'—a refusal to exert positive leadership at all levels to stop violent individuals from using the worst power imaginable." *Chris Lombardi, Correspondent, Women's E-News, New York City*

THE INSIDERS: A MAN'S RECOVERY FROM TRAUMATIC CHILDHOOD ABUSE by Robert Blackburn Knight. (2002). "An important book. . . . Fills a gap in the literature about healing from childhood sexual abuse by allowing us to hear, in undiluted terms, about one man's history and journey of recovery." *Amy Pine, MA, LMFT, psychotherapist and co-founder, Survivors Healing Center, Santa Cruz, California*

WE ARE NOT ALONE: A GUIDEBOOK FOR HELPING PROFESSIONALS AND PARENTS SUPPORTING ADOLESCENT VICTIMS OF SEXUAL ABUSE by Jade Christine Angelica. (2002). "Encourages victims and their families to participate in the system in an effort to heal from their victimization, seek justice, and hold offenders accountable for their crimes. An exceedingly vital training tool." *Janet Fine, MS, Director, Victim Witness Assistance Program and Children's Advocacy Center, Suffolk County District Attorney's Office, Boston*

WE ARE NOT ALONE: A TEENAGE GIRL'S PERSONAL ACCOUNT OF INCEST FROM DISCLOSURE THROUGH PROSECUTION AND TREATMENT by Jade Christine Angelica. (2002). "A valuable resource for teens who have been sexually abused and their parents. With compassion and eloquent prose, Angelica walks people through the criminal justice system—from disclosure to final outcome." *Kathleen Kendall-Tackett, PhD, Research Associate, Family Research Laboratory, University of New Hampshire, Durham*

WE ARE NOT ALONE: A TEENAGE BOY'S PERSONAL ACCOUNT OF CHILD SEXUAL ABUSE FROM DISCLOSURE THROUGH PROSECUTION AND TREATMENT by Jade Christine Angelica. (2002). "Inspires us to work harder to meet kids' needs, answer their questions, calm their fears, and protect them from their abusers and the system, which is often not designed to respond to them in a language they understand." *Kevin L. Ryle, JD, Assistant District Attorney, Middlesex, Massachusetts*

GROWING FREE: A MANUAL FOR SURVIVORS OF DOMESTIC VIO-LENCE by Wendy Susan Deaton and Michael Hertica. (2001). "This is a necessary book for anyone who is scared and starting to think about what it would take to 'grow free.' . . . Very helpful for friends and relatives of a person in a domestic violence situation. I recommend it highly." *Colleen Friend, LCSW, Field Work Consultant, UCLA Department of Social Welfare, School of Public Policy & Social Research*

A THERAPIST'S GUIDE TO GROWING FREE: A MANUAL FOR SUR-VIVORS OF DOMESTIC VIOLENCE by Wendy Susan Deaton and Michael Hertica. (2001). "An excellent synopsis of the theories and research behind the manual." *Beatrice Crofts Yorker, RN, JD, Professor of Nursing, Georgia State University, Decatur*

PATTERNS OF CHILD ABUSE: HOW DYSFUNCTIONAL TRANSACTIONS ARE REPLICATED IN INDIVIDUALS, FAMILIES, AND THE CHILD WELFARE SYSTEM by Michael Karson. (2001). "No one interested in what may well be the major public health epidemic of our time in terms of its long-term consequences for our society can afford to pass up the opportunity to read this enlightening work." *Howard Wolowitz, PhD, Professor Emeritus, Psychology Department, University of Michigan, Ann Arbor*

IDENTIFYING CHILD MOLESTERS: PREVENTING CHILD SEXUAL ABUSE BY RECOGNIZING THE PATTERNS OF THE OFFENDERS by Carla van Dam. (2000). "The definitive work on the subject. . . . Provides parents and others with the tools to recognize when and how to intervene." *Roger W. Wolfe, MA, Co-Director, N. W. Treatment Associates, Seattle, Washington*

POLITICAL VIOLENCE AND THE PALESTINIAN FAMILY: IMPLI-CATIONS FOR MENTAL HEALTH AND WELL-BEING by Vivian Khamis. (2000). "A valuable book . . . a pioneering work that fills a glaring gap in the study of Palestinian society." *Elia Zureik, Professor of Sociology, Queens University, Kingston, Ontario, Canada*

STOPPING THE VIOLENCE: A GROUP MODEL TO CHANGE MEN'S ABUSIVE ATTITUDES AND BEHAVIORS by David J. Decker. (1999). "A concise and thorough manual to assist clinicians in learning the causes and dynamics of domestic violence." *Joanne Kittel, MSW, LICSW, Yachats, Oregon*

STOPPING THE VIOLENCE: A GROUP MODEL TO CHANGE MEN'S ABUSIVE ATTITUDES AND BEHAVIORS, THE CLIENT WORKBOOK by David J. Decker. (1999).

BREAKING THE SILENCE: GROUP THERAPY FOR CHILDHOOD SEXUAL ABUSE, A PRACTITIONER'S MANUAL by Judith A. Margolin. (1999). "This book is an extremely valuable and well-written resource for all therapists working with adult survivors of child sexual abuse." *Esther Deblinger, PhD, Associate Professor of Clinical Psychiatry, University of Medicine and Dentistry of New Jersey School of Osteopathic Medicine*

"I NEVER TOLD ANYONE THIS BEFORE": MANAGING THE INITIAL DISCLOSURE OF SEXUAL ABUSE RE-COLLECTIONS by Janice A. Gasker. (1999). "Discusses the elements needed to create a safe, therapeutic environment and offers the practitioner a number of useful strategies for responding appropriately to client disclosure." *Roberta G. Sands, PhD, Associate Professor, University of Pennsylvania School of Social Work*

FROM SURVIVING TO THRIVING: A THERAPIST'S GUIDE TO STAGE II RECOVERY FOR SURVIVORS OF CHILDHOOD ABUSE by Mary Bratton. (1999). "A must read for all, including survivors. Bratton takes a lifelong debilitating disorder and unravels its intricacies in concise, succinct, and understandable language." *Phillip A. Whitner, PhD, Sr. Staff Counselor, University Counseling Center, The University of Toledo, Ohio*

SIBLING ABUSE TRAUMA: ASSESSMENT AND INTERVENTION STRATEGIES FOR CHILDREN, FAMILIES, AND ADULTS by John V. Caffaro and Allison Conn-Caffaro. (1998). "One area that has almost consistently been ignored in the research and writing on child maltreatment is the area of sibling abuse. This book is a welcome and required addition to the developing literature on abuse." *Judith L. Alpert, PhD, Professor of Applied Psychology, New York University*

BEARING WITNESS: VIOLENCE AND COLLECTIVE RESPONSIBILITY by Sandra L. Bloom and Michael Reichert. (1998). "A totally convincing argument. . . . Demands careful study by all elected representatives, the clergy, the mental health and medical professions, representatives of the media, and all those unwittingly involved in this repressive perpetuation and catastrophic global problem." *Harold I. Eist, MD, Past President, American Psychiatric Association*

TREATING CHILDREN WITH SEXUALLY ABUSIVE BEHAVIOR PROBLEMS: GUIDELINES FOR CHILD AND PARENT INTERVENTION by Jan Ellen Burton, Lucinda A. Rasmussen, Julie Bradshaw, Barbara J. Christopherson, and Steven C. Huke. (1998). "An extremely readable book that is well-documented and a mine of valuable 'hands on' information. . . . This is a book that all those who work with sexually abusive children or want to work with them must read." *Sharon K. Araji, PhD, Professor of Sociology, University of Alaska, Anchorage*

THE LEARNING ABOUT MYSELF (LAMS) PROGRAM FOR AT-RISK PARENTS: LEARNING FROM THE PAST—CHANGING THE FUTURE by Verna Rickard. (1998). "This program should be a part of the resource materials of every mental health professional trusted with the responsibility of working with 'at-risk' parents." *Terry King, PhD, Clinical Psychologist, Federal Bureau of Prisons, Catlettsburg, Kentucky*

THE LEARNING ABOUT MYSELF (LAMS) PROGRAM FOR AT-RISK PARENTS: HANDBOOK FOR GROUP PARTICIPANTS by Verna Rickard. (1998). "Not only is the LAMS program designed to be educational and build skills for future use, it is also fun!" *Martha Morrison Dore, PhD, Associate Professor of Social Work, Columbia University, New York*

BRIDGING WORLDS: UNDERSTANDING AND FACILITATING ADOLESCENT RECOVERY FROM THE TRAUMA OF ABUSE by Joycee Kennedy and Carol McCarthy. (1998). "An extraordinary survey of the history of child neglect and abuse in America. . . . A wonderful teaching tool at the university level, but should be required reading in high schools as well." *Florabel Kinsler, PhD, BCD, LCSW, Licensed Clinical Social Worker, Los Angeles, California*

CEDAR HOUSE: A MODEL CHILD ABUSE TREATMENT PROGRAM by Bobbi Kendig with Clara Lowry. (1998). "Kendig and Lowry truly . . . realize the saying that we are our brothers' keepers. Their spirit permeates this volume, and that spirit of caring is what always makes the difference for people in painful situations." *Hershel K. Swinger, PhD, Clinical Director, Children's Institute International, Los Angeles, California*

SEXUAL, PHYSICAL, AND EMOTIONAL ABUSE IN OUT-OF-HOME CARE: PREVENTION SKILLS FOR AT-RISK CHILDREN by Toni Cavanagh Johnson and Associates. (1997). "Professionals who make dispositional decisions or who are related to out-of-home care for children could benefit from reading and following the curriculum of this book with children in placements." *Issues in Child Abuse Accusations*

Order a copy of this book with this form or online at:
http://www.haworthpress.com/store/product.asp?sku=5488

A SAFE PLACE TO GROW
A Group Treatment Manual for Children in Conflicted, Violent, and Separating Homes

_____ in hardbound at $34.95 (ISBN-13: 978-0-7890-2768-9; ISBN-10: 0-7890-2768-2)

_____ in softbound at $22.95 (ISBN-13: 978-0-7890-2769-6; ISBN-10: 0-7890-2769-0)

Or order online and use special offer code HEC25 in the shopping cart.

COST OF BOOKS_____

POSTAGE & HANDLING_____
(US: $4.00 for first book & $1.50
for each additional book)
(Outside US: $5.00 for first book
& $2.00 for each additional book)

SUBTOTAL_____

IN CANADA: ADD 7% GST_____

STATE TAX_____
(NJ, NY, OH, MN, CA, IL, IN, PA, & SD
residents, add appropriate local sales tax)

FINAL TOTAL_____
(If paying in Canadian funds,
convert using the current
exchange rate, UNESCO
coupons welcome)

☐ **BILL ME LATER:** (Bill-me option is good on
US/Canada/Mexico orders only; not good to
jobbers, wholesalers, or subscription agencies.)
☐ Check here if billing address is different from
shipping address and attach purchase order and
billing address information.

Signature_____

☐ **PAYMENT ENCLOSED: $**_____

☐ **PLEASE CHARGE TO MY CREDIT CARD.**

☐ Visa ☐ MasterCard ☐ AmEx ☐ Discover
☐ Diner's Club ☐ Eurocard ☐ JCB

Account #_____

Exp. Date_____

Signature_____

Prices in US dollars and subject to change without notice.

NAME_____

INSTITUTION_____

ADDRESS_____

CITY_____

STATE/ZIP_____

COUNTRY_____ COUNTY (NY residents only)_____

TEL_____ FAX_____

E-MAIL_____

May we use your e-mail address for confirmations and other types of information? ☐ Yes ☐ No
We appreciate receiving your e-mail address and fax number. Haworth would like to e-mail or fax special
discount offers to you, as a preferred customer. **We will never share, rent, or exchange your e-mail address
or fax number.** We regard such actions as an invasion of your privacy.

Order From Your Local Bookstore or Directly From
The Haworth Press, Inc.
10 Alice Street, Binghamton, New York 13904-1580 • USA
TELEPHONE: 1-800-HAWORTH (1-800-429-6784) / Outside US/Canada: (607) 722-5857
FAX: 1-800-895-0582 / Outside US/Canada: (607) 771-0012
E-mail to: orders@haworthpress.com

For orders outside US and Canada, you may wish to order through your local
sales representative, distributor, or bookseller.
For information, see http://haworthpress.com/distributors

(Discounts are available for individual orders in US and Canada only, not booksellers/distributors.)

PLEASE PHOTOCOPY THIS FORM FOR YOUR PERSONAL USE.
http://www.HaworthPress.com   BOF04